Suicide
from the Other Side

Susan Rushing

Susan Rushing

Copyright © 2012 Susan Rushing

All rights reserved.

ISBN-10: 1479123838
ISBN-13: 978-1479123834

ACKNOWLEDGEMENTS

In this life, I've been given many angels, who walk the earth in human form. I will never be able to adequately express my gratitude for the gifts they have given to me. I dedicate this book to the love I have for each of them and for the love they have given so generously in return.

Sondra Landrum

Cynthia Campbell

Patti Starr

Candace Apple

Chip Coffey

Lenna Moore

Bob Moore

Clayton Fannin

Heather Herbee Lowe

Reba Ponder Weiss

Sue Anne Morgan

Megan Rushing

and

Brian Keith Rushing

Susan Rushing

CONTENTS

How to use this book

Introduction

1	Suicide According to the Great Collective "They"	1
2	"They" The Scholars	5
3	My Personal Religious "They"	13
4	The World's Religious "They"	19
5	The Legal "They"	35
6	The Social "They"	47
7	Prelude to the Other Side	61
8	The Gift	67
9	TripTik from the Universe	77
10	Grandfather Revisits	85
11	Encountering Souls	91
12	Chakra Khan, Let Me Love You	145
13	What Is Good Above Is Good Below	167

HOW TO USE THIS BOOK
AND A BIG DISCLAIMER

I had several people read the manuscript of this book, before I even thought to take it to print. Most of those people were smiling and glossy eyed when I handed them the stack of paper with all of these hard worked words upon the pages. They were happy to read it. I was grateful for them to take the time to do it. Most of those people didn't finish it. The ones who did, returned the manuscript back to me looking like I had hit them with a board. Some people just got plain old mad at me. After that kind of response, you would think I'd have put the thing in a drawer or the shredder and moved on. However, one person, who had been through the crisis of a good friend's suicide, came back to me after reading it with a somber look on her face. She handed the pages back to me and said, "This was hard, but it changed my life. Thank you for letting me read it." I hugged her and she hugged me back for a long time. In that moment, I knew this book did have value. It has value for those who are ready to heal. It has value for those who are willing to open their hearts and minds to the power of love. It has value for those who are willing to tear apart their lifelong belief systems and begin to understand the power of love. Love heals all.

Now, let me say right here ... I am blunt. I am blunt in this book. As I wrote it, I was angry and healing from my own battle with the suicide of my daughter's father. I tell my story of healing in this book. I tell about all of the paradigms that I had to rip through to be able to feel love again. I will also tell the stories of some people on the otherside who have chosen to end their own lives, and what it is like there, once the choice has been made. I am hoping that part will give your heart some ease.

You will get mad at me a few times, as I challenge you to re-examine your way of thinking. It's okay, get mad. Being mad will put a fire under you sometimes. I just ask that you please keep reading through your anger. I have things to tell you and show you, which will help you get through this. So, you go on and get mad at me. I'm just gonna love you through it. Hopefully by the end of this book, you will be doing the same for me and you and everyone else.

You will notice on the cover of this book is a dragon. In Chinese, the dragon symbolizes water. In dream analysis water symbolizes emotion. I talk about battling a dragon a great deal in this book. The dragon we battle is emotion. We can choose to fight for control over the dragon or we can choose to drown in the emotion. The choice is ours.

I choose to be a fighter. I think you should too.

    As I tell everyone who talks with me or takes one of my classes or workshops: You take what I have to give you. If it sounds right and feels right, then keep it. If I say something which doesn't feel right or rubs you in the wrong way, throw that part out. Don't throw the baby out with the bathwater. Keep the good, and get rid of the bad. This, boys and girls, is the first lesson in how to rebuild your belief systems to support yourself and everyone else in love.

It's all about the love.

Suicide from the Other Side

INTRODUCTION

"When life hands you lemons, make lemonade. That's what "they" say. Well, I say, "When life hands you lemons, you had better pray it hands you a lime and some tequila...because Sugar, you are going to need a cocktail." – Susan Rushing

I would like to approach the writing of this book in a calm and serene way. Because, those who go through this particular brand of ugliness need a little peace of mind.

We need someone to talk softly to us, pet our heads, wipe our eyes, and give us big love and warm hugs. Even though I am the softest, gushiest big-loving girl around, I am going to start this thing by saying out loud, with full lung capacity, and diaphragmatic thrust,

"SUICIDE IS BIG SUCK!"

There it is in all of its crappy truth. I don't apologize for it.

You hurt, I hurt and that pain reverberates through the earth every time it happens. Please bear with me; I will shed the bitterness in a minute.

But, as we start out, I really think it best for us to

get this negative part out of the way. I am a "tell it like it is" kind of girl. So, I will caution you to put on your seatbelt, your big girl panties, or your helmet... whatever you need to do to get through this. Don't be afraid to keep reading. At this moment, I am a sheep in wolves clothing. That is... I *was* a sheep, following blindly down the path of what I was told to believe and told to love and told to be afraid of. I had to get mad enough to fight my way to the top of this mess so I could find peace and forgiveness. If you are open in your heart and mind, I feel what I am about to tell you may give your heart some ease. What I hope it will do is allow you the ability to get fighting mad about this whole crock of crisis and then allow you to love everyone and yourself through it enough to allow yourself to heal.

Before we get down to it, I will tell you this; even though you may feel like it, you are most assuredly NOT alone. According to the CDC (Center for Disease Control) the suicide rate is increasing in the United States. In 2007, it was the 11th leading cause of death. In 2009, it was the 10th leading cause of death, with women attempting twice as often as men. The CDC calls it an insignificant rise. I got that bit of information from the CDC website, if you want to go and check it out for yourself. The CDC may not see the statistic as a big deal but I see it as a big sign. It is an obvious indication that times are hard and this fast paced world of high accountability and chemical ingestion is spinning more and more of us off the merry-go-round of life. That statistic feels pretty significant to this old girl.

My awareness of suicide began at an early age. I knew what the word suicide meant before I even started school, because my uncle Tommy committed suicide when I was very small.

My daddy had a younger sister named Delora. She fell in love with a good looking boy named Tommy and married young. I remember how they winked at each other and how playful they were together. They had a nice, ranch style house in Lexington, Kentucky. My aunt Delora was very pretty and stylish with her teased frosted hair and suntan. She decorated her house in an equally swanky 70's décor. I only remember visiting there a few times. But, when I go back to that house, in my mind, I picture everything wrapped in a layer of pastel velvet. In actuality, I more than likely saw just a single piece of furniture with velour upholstery, but at three or four, it looked mighty like Hollywood to me.

Behind the house was a big backyard. Delora took me back there once to show me a chicken she kept in a little, bitty chicken house. When we looked under the chicken, there was a little brown egg. Delora picked up the egg and took it back in the house with us. It was magic to me and I figured life couldn't be any more perfect than it was right there. Smiles and laughter were always in the air in that fabulous place.

I liked my uncle Tommy. He was tall and handsome as could be and so sweet to me. His black wavy hair shone with whatever kind of slick stuff he put in it every day. Tommy smiled big and winked a lot. He made me want to be a winker too. I remember, he thought it was the funniest thing ever that I could be so little and wink back at him. He would grin from ear to ear, pick me up and squeeze me hard whenever I winked. He was a charmer. I remember thinking, when someone said "tall dark and handsome" they had to be talking about my uncle Tommy. He sure was pretty.

A few years later, I heard Tommy had shot himself. I was shocked and stunned. I just couldn't believe it. My smiling uncle Tommy couldn't have been so sad. It didn't make sense. I cannot remember the particulars and reasons regarding my uncle Tommy's suicide, but I do remember how it rocked the family. I remember certain phrases like "closed casket" and "what a waste" being whispered quietly. Those whispers felt like black tissue paper floating through the air to me. Those whispers made me feel icky. I remember wanting to stop those people from whispering. I also remember how the whole ordeal aged my aunt Delora and how it changed her demeanor, forever.

 My next brush with suicide came at the age of ten or eleven. It was late afternoon; early evening was approaching. My mother, who was of the working variety of mothers, had just come to pick me up at my Aunt Judy's house. My mom and my aunt were sitting in the kitchen talking and I was in the living room watching a Carol Burnet Show rerun. Suddenly, the front door burst wide open and through it came the older lady who lived next door. Her face was almost purple and she was screaming, "Debbie's dead! She's killed herself!" My mom and aunt bolted from their chairs and ran to follow the woman out the front door. My mom hesitated only for a moment to yell, "Do not even think about coming out of this house".

It turned out; Debbie had shot herself in the stomach with a shotgun. She had put the butt of the gun on the floor and leaned into it to pull the trigger. Her boyfriend had just broken up with her earlier that day.

Debbie was seventeen. She lived next door with her grandma. I only knew her a little. I had seen her many times, around her house or on the porch of their house. She never had much to say to me. When I was friendly and spoke to her, she usually rolled her eyes and went inside. I figured it must be what teenager's were supposed to do, and went on my merry way, not taking it personally.

Despite my mother's warning, I did go outside the day Debbie died. I didn't venture from the house, but I did poke my head out of the screen-door. From the safety of the front porch, I saw my mother standing in the front yard next door with her hand over her mouth. My aunt Judy was holding up the sobbing grandmother. Poor Debbie was standing in the yard like she had no idea what was going on. The confusion on her fading face was palpable…and then she was gone. Once she had completely faded from view, I went back inside, plopped back down on the couch like I had never seen anything, which was always the best thing to do back then.

I see dead people. I have for as long as I can remember.

It was plenty confusing as a kid. But, today, I am a professional psychic and medium. It's what I do for a living. I have people sit in my office every day, asking to connect with loved ones who have crossed over. The majority of people I encounter have passed in normal ways. Heart attack, cancer, car accident ... those sorts of things are frequent. However, an unsettling trend began to be apparent a few years ago. It started with a request for a free reading from an event promoter. Of course, I was feeling all put-out to be asked to work without compensation. There was no way, in my fear-based, ego-soaked moment, that it even crossed my mind how I was being given a gift. The Universe delivers gifts in unusual wrappers and this one was no exception. This gift, this knowledge, is what I am about to share with you.

I was first shown this information in March of 2008. After that, readings for families affected by suicide became a specialty for me. My guides and angels offered a great deal of information in the form of visions and channeling, which I shared gladly, with each client. I was feeling pretty good about the information and the comfort I was able to bring to people. I said many gratitudes to the Universe, for allowing me to see this beautiful information. I wrote an article which was published in an online magazine about what I had seen, in hopes the information would be viewed by more and more people.

But, as the Universe decides, my knowing and seeing this information wasn't enough.

On May 19, 2010, my daughter's father went out into the garage, shut the door, and turned on the van. It rocked us all to our very foundation. I felt as though part of my energy had been taken. It kicked my feet out from under me. It still does. Is it getting better? Yes, gradually. I continue to have set backs and some days I don't think I will ever get through it. I felt like I was broken when it happened, like I would always be broken. Today, I realize I am not broken, and I really never was. Sometimes, when the Universe decides to make major changes in our world, it is hard for us on earth to adjust to the climate. The Universe changed its paradigm, and it was time for me to change my paradigm too…that is, if I was going to survive.

You have to reinvent your belief system. It is hard

and it takes a great deal of looking inward. If you picked up this book, you must be ready to start the process. The first thing we have to do is confront the facts of it.

Suicide happens. If it has happened to you and your loved ones, just claim it. Don't be embarrassed. It happened. You can't take it back and you can't hide it, if you are going to heal from it. Suicide isn't a stigma. It isn't something to hide. Suicide is a big ugly dragon, which you have been left to slay.

This very ugly dragon has so many tricks and magical powers up its scaly sleeves; there is little hope you will leave the battle unscathed. The fight will be hard and long. But, the beast can be beaten. Once the battle is done, don't look for any fairy tale treasure chest lying at your feet. There won't be one. It isn't that kind of battle. There is no reward. There is no princess to save. The only one to rescue will be you, and you will be changed. Not changed for the better, not changed for the worse, just changed, and that's okay. Really, it is.

When enough time has passed and you are able to view it from an outsider's perspective, you will realize, in the middle of this impossible chaos, the Universe had everything under control.

There was Divine order at that time and there is Divine order as you are living right now. It all happened exactly the way it was supposed to happen.

I know... you just gave me the silent finger. I understand fully your need to do so and I am loving you through the finger. Stay with me and read on. I am walking in the same shoes as you. I just have an inside track which I think might help.

My mission, in writing this book, is to give you the information I have been shown. And also, give you inspiration to heal and grow and try to find something positive in this terrible situation. I am doing this, right along with you. I hope to give you a safe place to cry and vent and heal. I want to help you find the order and purpose, in *your* monster of a circumstance. You can get better... and feel better... and be better... and love better... and understand better. I am hoping to shed a peaceful light on this dark chaos. You may get angry with me. You may not believe me but keep reading. Together, we will walk a path of love and healing. It can be tough. We are going to have to love one another through this. It's just I get to do all the talking. You can laugh a little, right here.

Susan Rushing

1

SUICIDE ACCORDING TO THE GREAT COLLECTIVE "THEY"

You know what they say.

Of course, you do! We all know what "they" say. "They" are always saying something. "They" have tons to say. In fact, "they" have something to say about everything, and every situation, which ever existed. "They" say plenty, and you and I both know it. We have heard people saying this little line over and over again throughout our lives.

We don't really know who "they" are, but we sure do pay attention to them when "they" say something. So, I thought we might begin looking at suicide from the "they" standpoint. We can talk about the views on suicide that "they" have. Heck, we can even take a look at some "they's" of varying cultures. What "they" say can be pretty interesting. It can be frustrating too. It can also be pretty enlightening and, it can also be positively indicative of the fear "they" try to keep us in so "they" can stay in control. Now this sounds a little scary, like some sort of conspiracy theory, right? Well, I suppose you can look at it like that if it makes it more intriguing. The reality is "they" have controlled our way of thinking for as long as "they" have been around.

Who the heck are "they" really? Well, "they" are a paradigm, an idea, a way of thinking, a thought form that has taken life. So, let's examine some of those ideas and ways of thinking and see where they fit into "OUR" paradigm. That's right; I said "our" paradigm, or even better yet, "YOUR" paradigm. After all, it's up to you how you are going to process this situation and get through it in a healthy way. Sometimes in order to heal we have to look deep inside of ourselves. It is hard work, but worth every little minute of it. It's time we develop our own Divinely guided ideas, our paradigm of love and forgiveness in the Christ consciousness, or whatever consciousness is in your paradigm. We are going to define what "we" say.

Digging up the belief systems of the past and rolling them around in our hands to take a good look at them can be difficult, but I will tell you right now....it is liberating, empowering and emancipating. So, get your boots on and grab your hard hat, boys and girls. Let's all get down with the excavation, we're going to blow the roof off this sucker...in the most loving and kindest way possible.

Susan Rushing

"THEY" – THE SCHOLARS

Sometimes, defining something is a good place to start. We look to other sources for validation and clarification of a word or an idea, so it's easier for us to wrap our heads around. So we can begin building our new belief system by taking a look at some other people's definitions and see how it makes us feel, and how it fits into how we are feeling.

Ok, so the first place we all go to for information these days is the internet. So let's start there with good old Wikipedia. Wiki shall be our first "they".

The Wiki definition for suicide is pretty factual, and I can respect it. I only want to beat it up a little. It goes a little something like this:

__Suicide__ (Latin suicidium, from suicaedere, "to kill oneself") is the act of a human being intentionally causing his or her own death. Suicide is often committed out of despair, or attributed to some underlying mental disorder which includes depression, bipolar disorder, schizophrenia, alcoholism and drug abuse. Pressures or misfortunes such as financial difficulties or troubles with interpersonal relationships may play a significant role.

I feel like the Wiki definition certainly speaks to the change in perspective of these times in comparison to our old school resource "Webster", of which we will talk about in just a minute. Now, I certainly don't agree with everything in the Wiki definition, but it seems to be a kinder and gentler definition over all. I do have a small issue with the "intention" part, which we will discuss later down the page when we dissect the Webster definition. Wiki does mention mental illness. We don't see any of that kind of forgiveness in

Webster. The Webster definition seems a little more rigid and straight laced; much like my mother in her best church suit.

So, let's move on to the Webster definition. I really want to bust this definition up. Whenever we rebuild or rehab anything, it is important to tear things apart so we can put them back together in a way which feels better and works better for us to be in a place of love. Webster is an old school paradigm, just as the view most of us have been taught of suicide is an old school paradigm.

The definition of the word "suicide" in the Webster's dictionary reads like this:

Suicide- a : *the act or an instance of taking one's own life voluntarily and intentionally especially by a person of years of discretion and of sound mind.*

Let's just take a quick look at this little ditty, and break it down into chunks we can examine very closely.

The first bit,

"the act or an instance of taking one's own life"

This is a verifiable statement and pretty much sums up what happened. I have no argument of that. So far, we are on the same page.

The next bit of text :

"voluntarily and intentionally"

Okay, I realize this seems like a perfectly accurate statement in regard to the situation, but personally, I have a little quarrel with it. As a medium, I have seen so many people who were thought to have killed themselves. One of the first things many of them say, when they come through is, "I messed up. I tried to back out but it was too late." Perhaps the intention to commit suicide was there in the beginning, but when push came to shove, the realization that dying wasn't really what they wanted to do came calling a little too late. I call those sorts of things "accidents". I know, the death certificate still says "suicide". I am here to tell you that many 'suicide victims" did not mean to complete the job. Take a minute to think about the last time you were very emotionally wrought or over the top angry. Did you ever do, or say, something in the emotion of the moment, you wish you could take back? Of course you have. So have I. I often know in the very moment of committing this form of disrespect, it is not in my greatest good to do it. Many times that thought doesn't cut through the fog of emotion to stop me until I have done the worst damage. Intention can change in an instant and a then a voluntary act can bring about an involuntary ending.

I am going to give you the example of my husband, Brian. Before I go any further, I feel I need to run a quick disclaimer.

I am going to talk about Brian and myself, and our situation, in this book. I will not lie to you and tell you that writing it, or putting it out there for everyone to look at, is easy. I want you all to know I love Brian and I miss him. I have also been mad as a hornet at him. It might seem, at times, I am a little too matter of fact about a great deal of this. Please do not perceive this as me being cold or disassociated but instead, know it has taken a great deal of heart-wrenching work and looking inside of myself to get to the point of being able to see his death from an outside perspective. At least, on most days I can look at it from an outside perspective. I am still healing.

Back to intention…
I know, without a doubt, in his last moments, Brian changed his mind. He changed it at the last minute. I also know he had been out to that garage before. It didn't take a psychic or a detective to figure it out. He had disengaged the garage door opener, so it would have been impossible to open it from inside the car.

It was clear, at least to me, Brian had been out there before and hit the button on the garage door opener to save himself, at the last minute. Did Brian have intention to end his life on that day? Yes, he did. He had intended to end it a few times, but he always hit the garage door opener and got out of it when the end became imminent. It was clearly visible this time he had gone out of his way to remove his safety net.

When we found him, the door to the van was open. He had fallen down between the van and the wall of the garage. He was headed toward the door. Brian did have a clear intention to end his life when he started out, but he changed his mind again, only this time it was too late leading to his involuntary ending.

The next words of text are:

"especially by a person of years of discretion and of sound mind."

This phrase makes me furrow my brow and shake my head. I am going to try my best to keep this section simple and just say <u>anyone</u> that gets to the absolute bottom of the depths of despair, cannot be held to discernment or discretion, and cannot be sound of mind. There is a glitch which occurs; a deep sadness that turns into disease. This is a disease of the emotion, a tiredness of the soul that goes on and on, with what seems like no ending. There is no sound mind. There is no discretion. These words do not belong in association with suicide, in my opinion. I have no idea how time or age relates to it either. Suicide doesn't affect a select group. The disease is the same whether you are young or old, rich or poor, male or female. There is no varying degree of suicide depending on the group. It is what it is, for everyone touched by it.

My belief is that for whatever the reason, or purpose, a person who commits suicide is ill. It is an invisible, un-diagnosable illness. It is as devastating as any other sickness. Even though we are calling this a sickness, you must remember, it is not contagious. This emotional illness is a thought form of negativity which turns on the producer of the thought and forms a disease. I do realize assisted suicide is different in discretion and discernment. But, I feel the similarity between the two breaks right down to disease. Sickness of the mind, soul or body, it is still disease.

Please keep in mind, if you feel you are slipping into a depression or an anger which you cannot control, it is time for you to seek help. We will talk more about that, later in the book. Just keep on loving yourself, and know that I'm loving you too, even though we have never met. It's all about the love. I believe that.

So, we've weighed in with a couple of scholars, let's move on to religion. I know…Oh Boy.

MY RELIGIOUS "THEY"

I grew up as a Baptist girl, in a small farming town in south central Ohio. My very conservative parents were heavily involved members of the local First Baptist Church. My mother was the church secretary and a Deaconess. My step-father was the church treasurer and a Deacon. Me? I was up there with the choir singing to Jesus, every Sunday. Well, singing to Jesus, scouting the congregation for sleeping people and occasionally listening to a sweating preacher shouting opinions about the bible and pounding a wooden pulpit with his large heavy fists.

Back in those days, I bought every word he was selling, with every drop of sweat and every fist to wood. It had to be right, because he said so, because my parents said so, and because they all said so. These days, I don't put a great deal of stock into the religion they were preaching to us back then. But, I do still sing to my Jesus. Jesus has always been the real love for me. He lived it, he walked it, and he talked it. Love and forgiveness was his message. It is the spirituality which has always sounded best to me. It is the same spirituality that has seen me through raising a handicapped daughter and the suicide of her father. I speak that brand of spirituality to whoever will sit still long enough to hear me. It is the real thing, and really the only real thing.

The church of my childhood, and of my parents, was very clear on the ramifications of Suicide. There was no doubt and no confusion of any kind, if you took your own life you were headed straight into the fires of hell. There was no question. There was no discussion. I heard it plenty of times and learned that fact early on.

I remember with crystal clarity a school assembly I attended, when I was in junior high. In my memory, it is as if it happened just last week. I was 13, or so, sitting in a dark auditorium with all of my giggly, fidgety girlfriends. We were passing notes and trying to make one another laugh. The assembly began with a group of young performers singing and dancing. They opened with a grand production number. We were enthralled. They told jokes and squirted water out into the audience. We thought it was about the best assembly we had ever had. As we were leaving the auditorium, the performers were handing out little flyers. And, they personally made contact with each of us, asking us to come to their evening performance.

Of course, we begged our parents to take us to the show. Once we were there, we noticed the songs were not the kinds of songs they had sung at the assembly. These new songs were religious in nature. That was okay by me. I was cool with that. However, the coolness faded in the final part of the show. The cast began talking about teen suicide, and how killing yourself was a one way ticket to hell. Their straight toothed, snow white smiles had turned into sad, sorrowful faces. They expressed how they felt so badly, and so sorry for teens who took their own lives. Then, they played over the speaker system, a teen-aged boy's final recording.

He was sad, at his wits end, and apologizing for the failure he had been to his friends and parents. His girlfriend didn't care about him anymore and he had stopped caring about himself. At the end of his speech, there was a long pause and then a loud bang. It startled us all and somebody even screamed. Then, the lights came up and a young cast member stood in a single spotlight and stated, "That poor boy is now burning, forever, in hell. That's what happens when you decide to take your own life. You burn in hell." I still remember the horror I felt and the scenario, which played in my mind, of this poor boy lying in his room ... dead. I worried about the hysteria of his parents finding him there, in that state.

So, needless to say, they made their point. I remember thinking, even at that age, what a disappointment that God would not take mercy on the sad young man. I bought what they sold, that night. But, deep down inside, it didn't feel right. Here I sit 30 years later, knowing I was right. I was so right. I pray the boy in that recording (even though I think it was a fake) has found peace, and love, and also knows I forgive him, for scaring me half to death. Also, how glad I am that his cast mate was so wrong about his future.

Just an end note to this story: Once the show was over, the cast took us in small groups into different parts of the school. They asked if we had bibles and if we went to church. They sent us home with fear in our hearts and the feeling that we all needed to go to church. We needed to pray for our junior high sins, at the Gregg Street Church. To be precise; the Gregg Street church which later became the massive "Heritage Church", which sits on the edge of town and judges all who enter with their unreasonably judgmental, changeable-letter sign.

Susan Rushing

THE WORLD'S RELIGIOUS "THEY"

Now that we have looked at MY religious "They", (I am an only child, after all, I HAD to go first) let's move around the world a little. Remember we are looking for common threads and what resonates with us or rather what resonates with you. Find what feels good and keep it, just keep in mind a lot of PEOPLE have come between the spirit and the religion. You have the right to come to your own conclusions about these things, just like the people who wrote these religious ideas a long, long time ago. Also, please remember in most cases, the stories and lessons of ancient religions were kept on scrolls and from what I have read, scrolls are mighty heavy and a pain to pack around. In many cultures, spiritual leaders or followers, whatever the case may be, were taught to memorize what was written in those texts. As we know, some folks are just better at remembering, and some folks are better story tellers than others. You do your own research, if your gut tickles you to do so. I am just going to present what I have found in my research. *Disclaimer- Helmets and waders may be needed for this bit of the excavation.

Christianity

I am going to start with Christianity, mostly because I know more about this one and also because in the pie chart of world religions, Christianity takes up the biggest slice. So, in true Baptist form I am going to run long on this. I will try to make it as entertaining as possible. You know, throw in a little passion for effect. I will probably need to wipe my brow midway through. But, I've got a nice white, cotton hankie that will do the job nicely. Feel free to shout an "amen" or a "hallelujah", if you so desire. It might make you feel good. And, it will for sure make me feel more at home.

With all that being said…let's all head down to the river.

I figure the Christian "They" pretty much have one standard reference book on their religion. So, that is where I went first; The King James version of the Bible or as it is known in theology circles as the "KJV". Personally, the "KJV" is not my choice for spiritual guidance. Now, don't judge me yet. Give me a minute to explain. It seems to me that the KJV more like a good book to learn lessons from but not an actual manual for living. After all, these are stories are history at best, reworked and retold by men, until they fit the paradigm of a religion. For the real spiritual guidance, I always turn to my faith in God and my Jesus for that, not a man and a book. Jesus taught us to love unconditionally, and without grudge or judgment. He was a great healer of souls and bodies, and showed us that love is the greatest energy of all. I can get behind the kindness and peace of that kind of energy. Still, the bible is an interesting reading and we will find some things that will tickle our brains. In fact, you may be interested in what I found out about suicide, while perusing the written word.

The word "Suicide" is not found in the bible. Yeah,

I know, it surprised me too. The word "suicide" comes from the Latin "sui", meaning "oneself", and "cida", meaning to "to kill". Even though the actual verbiage is not found in the bible, there are plenty of references to the act. In fact, there are seven suicides cited in the good book.

When I began doing research for this book, I thought it was pretty darned synchronistic that there were 7 suicides listed. It seems the number 7 is a biggie in the Bible. So, of course, I had to look that up too. I always felt the number 7 was a reference to divine perfection, in the bible. You know: seven levels of heaven, seven loaves, seven fishes, seven days of Genesis, that sort of thing. Suicide doesn't sing the same divinely perfect song to me. But, as I researched, it became clear to me, for every perfect 7 there is a not so perfect seven. The message in this is about balance. In the metaphysical community, we like to call it Duality versus Singularity. It's about understanding all sides of everything, accepting them and loving them. I mean, those biblical folks had to have those seven years of famine to recognize what those seven years of plenty were about. A man falleth seven times to riseth up again, in Proverbs.

The universe loves to preach this message of living in wholeness or oneness, or singularity, so I am going to help it along. Mainly, because I like to preach it too. It helps with things like guilt and anger. It also helps explain things about situations and people we have trouble wrapping our heads around. It can help you define your new way of thinking. It is a good measuring system for everything. Let me tell you what I mean.

Duality/Singularity is best explained as the dance of opposites which occurs in absolutely everything. It goes a little like this: for every one thing there must be an equal and opposite thing. For instance, we can't have happiness without sadness. The sadness defines the happiness, and the happiness defines that sadness. You can't have one without the other.

The same is true for good and evil. You cannot have one without the other to define and challenge it. Love your goodness and then be grateful for your badness, as well. It is that same badness which defines your goodness.

The badness is what can help you become a much better person, once you identify it. Acknowledge those things you do which maybe aren't so pretty. Claim the ugliness, and then if it bothers you to look at it, make some changes.

Look into living in singularity, or wholeness. It is about acknowledging all sides of ourselves and loving ourselves, in totality. By looking at all sides of ourselves, we are able to own the parts which are more negative. And, if you don't like those characteristics, the goodness of you can make the appropriate adjustments without any guilt or apology. You know your poison. You know your antidote, I always say. It really holds true for every situation. It is best to examine and acknowledge all sides of every situation, to help you gain clearer perspective. It allows you to take a step outside and look at things from a distance.

Even though the word "suicide" is not in the Bible, and we don't actually get the full view of suicide, from those seven tragic Bible stories. There are some strong references to the deed. They are a little bit confusing. Because we all think we are pretty clear on the Christian view of suicide. But, really, there are more layers to dig through. Let's get to digging.

The Conservative Protestants (Baptists, Pentecostals etc.) will preach, with a mighty passion, just short of dancing, that suicide is self-murder. So, anyone who commits it is big sinning, and it is the same big sin as if the person murdered another human being.

The argument I have heard, from most conservative Protestants, is asking for salvation and accepting Jesus Christ as your personal savior has to be done prior to death. The problem with suicide is that once dead, an individual is unable to accept salvation. The unpardonable sin then becomes, not the suicide itself, but rather the refusal of the gift of salvation.

As we take a look back at the KJV reference book, the view of scripture is, once a person comes to faith in Jesus Christ, every sin they will ever commit is paid for (1 John 1;7), and "there is now NO condemnation for those who are in Christ Jesus"(Romans 8;1.) These Christians believe suicide to be a sin but do not believe it is impossible to find salvation. (Romans 4;8). However, Judas, who committed suicide in despair, is generally believed to have been damned. I wonder if Judas was forgiven. I mean, that would be a very Christ like thing to do. Maybe, we are all just a little angry at Judas, for ratting on our Jesus. I like to think Jesus was way bigger on love, than holding a grudge. That's just my opinion and having said it, let's move on to Rome and weigh in with the Vatican.

Catholics, when talking about suicide, say words

like "grievous sin". Their whole standpoint is based on the belief that your soul belongs to God. And, that you and your soul were a gift given, from Him, to the world. I know several precious people, who also subscribe to the whole "they are a gift to the world" thing. I am loving them through it. Really, I am.

Catholic's believe to take away a gift God has given is overstepping God's authority. We all know going over any boss' head is often bad news. However, I did find the Catechism of the Catholic Church, Number 2283 states: "We should not despair of the eternal salvation of persons who have taken their own lives. By ways known to him alone, God can provide the opportunity for salutary repentance. The Church prays for persons who have taken their own lives."

That all sounds, to me, like you DO have the option of forgiveness once suicide has been committed. It doesn't sound like fiery pits await anyone. No, there seems to be a loophole. Loopholes for forgiveness, that is all about the love right there.

Orthodox Christians, don't really make a firm statement on the subject. There have been those in the history of the Church who have killed themselves rather than be tortured and demoralized by invaders. They do not condemn those folks for it. They also feel suicide victims are most likely "not in their right minds" and that God will have mercy on them. In any case the EOC's leave the fate of suicides up to God, and avoid making judgment. Christians who avoid making judgment; I can definitely get behind that.

Bottom line: Christians believe suicide is a sin. But, all sins are forgiven, to those who ask forgiveness in Christ's name. And that, ladies and gentlemen, is why Jesus is the only man from whom I seek spiritual guidance.

I am adding a verse from John, I feel says it all.

"My sheep hear My voice, and I know them, and they follow Me. And I give them eternal life, and they shall never perish; neither shall anyone snatch them out of My hand. My Father, who has given them to Me, is greater than all; and no one is able to snatch them out of My Father's hand." - John 10:27-29

Judaism - Jewish law forbids suicide. It forbids it so much that it is not even viewed as an acceptable alternative if someone is being forced to commit another cardinal sin against another person. So basically, it is better to take someone else's life, rather than your own, if you are being forced to choose. If you assist someone in a suicide, you are also in some spiritual hot water. Don't ask someone to assist you either. It is the same sin, even if you hire it done.

Bottom line: Suicide is an unforgivable sin

Hinduism - There are as many views on suicide as Shiva has arms, in Hinduism. But, it is basically big taboo. Committing suicide is considered an act against the code of "Ahimsa". In case you are wondering what this mysterious code of Ahimsa is…well, it basically means you should be nice, kind and love-filled with no violence toward any living thing. That means ALL living things, people, animals, birds, and bugs. Yes, I said "bugs".

I did not follow the code of Ahimsa yesterday, when I ordered the execution of a spider which was crawling dangerously near me.

The belief behind Ahimsa is that all living things are connected. We are all just one big pot of cosmic energy, all connected, and all-loving, and that is all right. So, in general, committing suicide is a violation of the code and like the views of the conservative Christians is the same big giant sin as murdering someone. Some Hindu scripture states dying by suicide, or really any kind of violent death will result in becoming a ghost, causing you to wander the earth until the actual expiration date of the contract you agreed upon, and cosmically signed, with the folks upstairs before you were born.

However, there is some fine print that's worth reading. It states that Hinduism accepts a person's right to end one's life through the non-violent practice of fasting to death. This method is called Prayopayesa. Please, go on to read the even smaller print which reads Prayopayvesa is strongly restricted to people who have no desire or ambition left and no responsibilities left in this life.

Bottom Line: Suicide is violence against a living thing and although not unforgivable it is spiritually hard-time walking.

Islam - When I looked into the views of suicide in accordance to the Islam religion, I have to tell you, I was a little shocked. If there is a solid, iron clad statement on suicide, from any religion, it lies here with the Muslim people.

Islam's final answer is that suicide is one of the greatest sins and utterly detrimental to one's spiritual journey. In fact, it is called-out specifically in a verse in the fourth chapter of the Qur'an, An-Nisaa (The Woman) instructs; "And do not kill yourselves, surely God is most Merciful to you." (4:29)

Most Muslim scholars and clerics denounce all suicide, including suicide bombings, and frequently make reference to this verse, as a clear commandment forbidding the deed. This makes me wonder, and ponder, if Al Qaida is just a religious cult with political motives.

Bottom Line: Suicide for any reason is unforgivable.

Jainism - Jainism is a big religion that actually does accept suicides. Jain munis have been known to starve themselves to death, through what is considered a non-violent act called Santhara, which is fasting to death. Although taking one's own life is acceptable in this religion, there is a very strong insistence on non-violent behavior. This religion gives me shades of Buddhism. So…let's wander over to the Buddhists.

Buddhism - Looking inward for the answer, this is what the Buddhists teach us. It is not a : "We are going to tell you what you're going to do" religion. Don't get me wrong, there are guidelines. But, it all really boils down to Karma. That's what it's all about.

The intentional action of any one of the big three (body, mind, spirit) heavily effects the future. Basically your past action creates your present experiences and your present action creates your future.

Buddhism teaches that all people experience substantial suffering or "dukkah". This suffering comes from past negative actions. One of the most important and first lessons in Buddhism is to hold life in high regard. So, I am thinking, the destruction of life, including your own life, is most assuredly considered to be a negative action.

Some Buddhists believe if one takes one's own life, the person will repeat the negative action of the suicide every 7 days until the opportunity to reincarnate becomes available. Then, the soul should live out the next life and die naturally. Buddhism does not actually condemn suicide, like other religions. I suppose it would be bad Karma to go around condemning things.

However, suicide is clearly regarded as a "no-no", in the most loving and gentle way possible.

One interesting aspect, of this religion, is that some Buddhists believe suicide is appropriate and acceptable, as self-sacrifice for those who have attained enlightenment. However, this is very much an exception to the general belief.

Bottom Line: Suicide can be bad spiritual karma, unless you are self-sacrificing for further enlightenment.

Religious Cults – Heaven's Gate, Jim Jones…we remember these stories. We all still caution one another not to "drink the kool-aid", jokingly or not. Some religious cults not only accept suicide as appropriate, but actually persuade and encourage their members to take their own lives to provide the soul an escape route to a better world.

Bottom Line: With a cult, the bottom line is hazy. Sometimes, suicide becomes more than okay; it becomes a way to transcend.

Suzy says the bottom line is: *"Don't join a cult."*

You can see, from just this small cross section, the religious views of suicide are as plentiful as there are kinds of people on this earth. You should understand you have a right to your own belief here. Have faith in your God. Have faith in your higher self. Ask yourself what feels right to you, in your soul, regarding this.

I know, as a mother, my daughter could do just about anything to me and I would never stop loving her. I have to feel God loves so much greater than I can imagine. I can't think he would turn his back on one of his children. I know he wouldn't. Of course, that is my belief system, my paradigm.

Susan Rushing

THE LEGAL "THEY"

The legalities of suicide are difficult. In the past, various states listed the act of suicide as a felony, but as you can imagine, these laws were difficult to enforce. By the 1970s, eighteen U.S. states had done away with laws against suicide. As our social climate grew softer in the 1990's, thirty of the fifty states had no laws against suicide or suicide attempts but every state had laws declaring it to be felony to aid, advise or encourage another person to commit suicide.

The turn of the century showed only two states had laws against suicide, recognizing it as more of a psychological emergency rather than a crime. However, in some U.S. states, suicide is still considered an unwritten "common law crime". Basically the whole "common law crime" is about law suits. Suicide can make it difficult to get a settlement for the late suicidal person's family in a lawsuit unless the suicidal person can be proven to have been "of unsound mind." That means the suicide must be proven to have been an involuntary act of the victim in order for the family to be awarded monetary damages by the court. I know what you are thinking. How can it be that suicide can be proven to be involuntary when the very definition of suicide is all about the voluntary act of killing one's self, right? Well, these kinds of law suits have been filed in the case of negligent caregivers or a non vigilant security person at a jail or a hospital who was supposed to be supervising the deceased victim. One example would be the distraught person on trial for a crime who hangs himself in his cell.

When the suicide happens at home, the police are usually the first to arrive. I have heard some horror stories from mourning families about the insensitivity of law officials during their time of horrific crisis. I will tell you, my experience, for the most part, was not horrific. The policemen who arrived at the scene were professional, maybe a little brusque and direct, but nothing I couldn't handle. They walked around and asked a lot of sensitive questions and made a lot of loud and obnoxious statements. The detective who arrived was a different story. He was a tall, larger man with a concerned look on his face. He did his job and asked the questions he needed to ask. When I asked if I could leave the scene, his concerned look grew heavier and he asked me if I could wait for him to walk me out to my car. While we walked, he stayed close beside me with his arm outstretched so that his jacket blocked the view. I hadn't realized they were moving Brian's body into the ambulance at that very moment. The detective pulled me closer to him and said to me, "Just walk beside me and keep looking forward. You don't want to see this."

    I did as he said. Because, I knew he was right. I didn't want the sight of it. I am grateful for his sensitivity to me on that night. The Universe sends angels in many forms and at unexpected times, I know this to be true. On that terrible night, the detective was a comfort and a protection and a very tall angel for me. I will never forget it, or him and I will always be grateful.

They took Brian's body in for an autopsy, on that night. Yes, that very night, because that's what they do in Ohio. I am always amazed at clients who come in for readings and tell me they aren't sure if their loved one actually meant to die, or if the death was actually from natural causes, or if it was an accident. The first question I always ask is: "Wasn't there an autopsy?" It almost always shocks me.

Where I am from, in Ohio, when a person dies and the cause is not immediately apparent, they do an autopsy. Ohioans want to know what, where, why and how someone died, and they want scientific proof. They don't want some random person making that important call. They don't want a decision made without some kind of verifiable proof. It has been a different story in the south (Georgia), and the pseudo-south (Kentucky). I have had many people sit in front of me and ask me to connect with their loved one to find out what, exactly, happened.

Very often, the death certificate comes back marked suicide. Even though there was no note, no sign of sadness, and not a single clue to explain a motive for it, no autopsy was ever requested. Being left with no answers is a confusing and saddening place to be. It is an even sadder place when someone made the decision for you, your loved one, and your family. Knowing the truth gives you a starting place, to begin healing.

The word "suicide" on a death certificate is certainly a startling thing to see. It is amazing how much power a little word on a piece of paper can hold. I remember vividly, the day Brian's death certificate came in the mail. When I saw the envelope in the mailbox, I immediately got dizzy. It was like I was having some kind of weird little panic attack. I didn't want to open that envelope. I didn't really want to read it. I didn't want, or need, to see the cause of death.

After all, he came to me that night, when I got home. The way he appeared had confirmed it. Brian had, in fact, taken his own life.

After standing there, at the mailbox, for what seemed like forever, I finally managed to go inside with the envelope. I sat at the dining room table, opened it and took out the papers which were folded inside. As I read down the certificate with all of his vital information, my eyes finally rested on the "cause of death box". Written in that box was the word I knew would be there. But, still, I did not want to see…"suicide". It was official.

I sat in all my guilt and sorrow and stared at the word until it looked like it was growing out of the page. I wanted to hold that paper close to me so no one could see it. Not for me, but for Brian and our daughter. I didn't want people talking about it, shaking their heads, and whispering their opinions.

But, as much as I wanted to, I couldn't hide it. No one would let it be hidden. People around me waited intently for the final verdict. Like that little type written word was the gospel truth. Simply because, someone who didn't even know us had written a word, on a form, in black and white. Family and friends asked me all the time if I had gotten the death certificate yet. It agitated me. When I got it, they couldn't wait to ask the cause of death. It was like they couldn't hear anything else I had said, their ears trained only on that little ugly verdict. It made me angry. I got ugly with them. I figured they should just go back to watching their cable television and leave the real people alone. Our lives were not an episode of CSI. We weren't characters in some television drama or mystery series.

You know, I think I may have actually said that very thing to one or two people. I wasn't very nice about it, However, I am not apologizing. Sometimes, folks need a love tap on their forehead when they are being insensitive.

Let me step out of emotion here for a minute and get back to the legal thing.

One of the really basic ugly happenstances, or as I like to call them "crappenstances", which comes with suicide is that it very often nullifies the life insurance. That verdict, that little word on paper, is wielding its power again. So, there you sit, in all of your panic, sorrow, guilt, disbelief, anger, and confusion. Then, those folks who have claimed to be your "good neighbor" or told you how you are "in good hands", tell you in an impersonal and uncaring letter how even though you have been giving them money, every month, for final expenses, they can't hold up their end of the agreement because of the little "S word" on the death certificate. Suddenly, your good neighbor has built a bad fence.

Now what do you do? It isn't your fault. It wasn't your decision. But, you are left to deal with it.

Suicide is a disease. However, unlike cancer or heart disease, this sickness is completely disregarded as such, legally. This is another part of the dragon you have to slay. Battling insurance companies or retirement agencies during your grieving time can take a terrible toll on you. These people, whom you must now fight, are trained to deal with emotional people. They will seem not to care. They will seem not to want to deal with you. This is how they have been trained to act. Please don't take it personally.

Try to keep in mind; those same uncaring people have the same insurance company you do. Karma is the ultimate scorekeeper.

Assisted Suicide

We can't talk about the legal aspects of suicide without covering assisted suicide. I remember, back in the 1990's, all of the talk and big eyes over Dr. Kevorkian, and the news of him assisting terminally ill people in ending their battles. Some states immediately flew around making laws against it. Some American legal scholars began stepping forward and even the ACLU got involved. Their take on the issue was that denying someone the right to end their life was taking away a personal liberty. Former President of the ACLU, Nadine Strossen commented, "The idea of government making determinations about how you end your life, forcing you...could be considered cruel and unusual punishment in certain circumstances".

Physician-assisted suicide is legal in some states. On October 27, 1997, Oregon enacted the Death with Dignity Act, which allows terminally-ill Oregonians to end their lives through the voluntary self-administration of lethal medications, expressly prescribed by a physician for that purpose. The Oregon Death with Dignity Act requires the Oregon Department of Human Services to collect information about the patients and physicians who participate in the Act and publish an annual statistical report.

In Washington State, it became legal in 2009 when a law modeled after the Oregon act, the Washington Death with Dignity Act, was passed. A patient must be diagnosed as having less than six months to live, be of sound mind, make a request orally and in writing, have it approved by two different doctors, then wait 15 days and make the request again. A doctor may prescribe a lethal dose but may not administer it.

Currently, 34 STATES have statutes explicitly criminalizing assisted suicide: Alaska, Arizona, Arkansas, California, Colorado, Connecticut, Delaware, Florida, Georgia, Hawaii, Illinois, Indiana, Iowa, Kansas, Kentucky, Louisiana, Maine, Minnesota, Mississippi, Missouri, Montana, Nebraska, New Hampshire, New Jersey, New Mexico, New York, North Dakota, Oklahoma, Pennsylvania, Rhode Island, South Dakota, Tennessee, Texas and Wisconsin.

NINE states criminalize assisted suicide through common law. They are as follows: Alabama, Idaho, Maryland, Massachusetts, Michigan, Nevada, South Carolina, Vermont, and West Virginia.

THREE states have abolished the common law of crimes and do not have statutes criminalizing assisted suicide: North Carolina, Utah and Wyoming.

In Ohio, the state's Supreme Court ruled, in October 1996, assisted suicide is not a crime.

In Virginia, there is no real clear case law on assisted suicide, nor is there is a statute criminalizing the act, although there is a statute which imposes civil sanctions on persons assisting in a suicide.

Only the states of Oregon and Washington permit physician-assisted suicide.

Source: Associated Press. Provided by Infonet

Susan Rushing

THE SOCIAL "THEY"

As I began to write this section, I found myself with my hands to my face and taking deep breaths. The social aspects of suicide are tricky and sick making for me. I have been through some hard things in my life. People can be so hard on one another. What I have found is that even those you hold closest to you will disappoint you. No matter who they are or what they are, to you, there are three things which hold true in this life:

1. People love to judge.
2. People love scandal.
3. People love to talk judgment and scandal.

I ask you; why else would these reality television shows be such big hits?

When Brian committed suicide, I couldn't believe the cold comments and insensitive remarks and questions people brought to me. Most of these crazy remarks and questions came from my closest friends and family members. More than a few times, I sat back in amazement at the harshness that came out so easily. It almost seemed like things were being said to me just to see how I would react. It was painful coming from those I trusted most.

Brian and I were legally married for 22 years. We spent the first nine years in the same house and slept in the same bed. In that time together, we had a daughter. She was born prematurely and was critically ill. For two months, we sat together every day in a neonatal intensive care unit praying, rocking and singing to our baby. We celebrated, together, when she finally came home. We worried and laughed and played with her, together, everyday.

She is severely handicapped. We went through three brain surgeries, countless seizures and dozens of hospital stays, together. We went through a great deal of crisis, together. I saw him every weekend when he came to pick up Megan for visitation. We talked a couple of times each week. We made decisions for our daughter, together. We were in that relationship for 22 years, together.

It shocked me, to my foundation, when I heard people comment on how I shouldn't have been so upset. After all, we had "been split up" for years. It stung, when I was a sideline mention in his obituary. It didn't surprise me, really. During the many dramatic moments of my life, there have always been those people, whom I loved and counted on for support, who never hesitated to express their opinion. They always made sure I knew what it was, whether it was harsh and hurtful, or not. Has all of this made me bitter and hateful? Well, I will tell you that I started to let it get to me when Megan was still very small. Thankfully, I started seeing the detriment caused by negative energy. Anger and resentment are like a knife with no handle. You may use it to jab at other people but you wind up cutting yourself just as badly. I just started trying to love myself enough to take a lesson in it all.

Crisis has defined many relationships for me. So, I came up with a theory about relationships. I call it the "Tree Theory of Relationships". The title isn't very witty, I know, but the theory is helpful and I want to share it with you. I used to reserve this theory only for friends. Since Brian's death, I have found that family, even the closest ones, will fall squarely into one of the categories of this theory.

The Tree Theory goes something like this:
People in your life are like parts of a tree:

Leaf People

The leaf people in your life are around when the weather is nice. They are nice to have around and the make you smile to look at them. Leaf people may give you some protection and keep you cool, but leaf people will fall off when the weather turns or blow off, if it gets too windy. You will have a ton of leaf people in your life. Enjoy leaf people while they are around. They are fun while they last, and who knows, they may grow back in another season.

Twig People

Twig people will hang around a lot longer than a leaf person. They will stick around through a season change. Well, as long as you don't put any pressure on them. A twig person cannot support you. You can bet they will break away when a storm comes through. Twig People will be plentiful in your life. Love them for who they are. They try and do the best they can, they just aren't very strong.

Branch People

Branch people are pretty dependable. They will hold you up and you can lean on them without worry. Unless, it is particularly bad weather or the wind really blows hard. A branch person will reluctantly break away in a storm and still leave you. Branch People are good to have in your life. If you have several branch friends, you can call yourself lucky. Just don't hang on them or pull too hard, they may snap.

Trunk People

You can't get too much better than a trunk person. A trunk person will be strong when the weather is bad. They will bend and sway to support you. They will let you hang on to them and they will support you through a great deal. They won't mind if you lean on them, hug them or even carve your name on them. However, someone could come along and cut the trunk person out of your life. Lightening of some sort could strike that trunk and cause it to split. If you have a few trunk people in your life you will be fine. They will love you and support you through all kinds of weather. Well, except lightening and other people.

Root People

Root people, wow. You only get one or two root people in your whole life. You will know who they are. You may be thinking of one right now. Root people are strong. They will be with you and dig their feet in for you. You can sit on them or lean on them or hang on through the bitterest of storms, and root people will stay planted. These people are few and far between. These are the people who love you through it all. They don't ever leave. They are *always* there, beneath the surface, staying true and grounded.

It may be important for you to define the people who surround you. For me, it has been a good way to keep things in perspective. The tree theory allows me to look at myself and see where I am on other people's trees. It helps me to be more accountable, for the way I respond and care for my friends and family ... and also, for myself. When I started looking at my own tree, I discovered the biggest epiphany of all. You don't leave your tree, ever. You always have the tree. If you treat the tree badly, it will be sick. It will be weak. If you don't nourish the tree, YOU are the one who suffers. You may use your tree to hold other people up. But, if you don't care for that tree, it can't be supportive in any way ... to anyone. Keeping your tree healthy is the key. It is the most important task. The relationship with yourself is the most important thing you have. I know it might sound selfish but it really isn't. That particular idea is a pretty tough one for most people to wrap their heads, and hearts, around. But, you need to believe it. It is the rock solid truth, and a mighty weapon to gain for your dragon slaying.

You will love a good many people in your life and a good many people will love you right back. In all of this wonderful loving there is a hard fact in it. People will leave you. People are transient like that, even if they don't want to leave you or don't make a conscious choice to leave you, they still can. Enjoy them and love them well while they are with you. Other people are temporary.

You, however, are what you have, forever. You are the one who stays with you through it all. You were there when you took your first breath and you will be there with you when you take your last breath. You have You. So, it seems to me this relationship is the most important one you will ever have. If your tree of self is in crisis, there is no way it can support anyone else.

If you are supporting and loving yourself in real and honest ways, you will be better equipped to protect yourself from the judgment of other people. The insensitivity will still shock you, no doubt. You will find if you truly understand yourself and have your own back, you will get through it much more easily. I have struggled, and struggled, to understand the motives and thinking of the people who were so careless in those days right after Brian's suicide. The only thing I can guess is that a good many people must be nearsighted; nearsighted in a way which causes the inability to look past the three foot distance of their own personal space.

I have found that sometimes, people get so wrapped up in what is going on in their own front yards, they never bother to take a look at what someone else might have going on in a neighboring yard. Chances are, they don't even think about all that is swirling around in your head and how what they say could possibly affect you. Maybe, they don't have enough self value to even understand how little old them could say or do anything to make an impact on anyone. Whatever the reason, you are going to have to love them through it and make sure you put a heaping helping of that love back on yourself. I know you just gave me another silent finger. I totally understand how it is difficult to love someone when they are beating the tar out of you, emotionally. You have to do it. Try to understand that as you love this person, you love yourself right back. Now, let me also say it is not okay to allow someone to abuse you or to continuously make you feel devalued, disrespected or compromised. It is perfectly fine and completely acceptable to love someone from a distance. Your number one concern is to take care of you.

    This understanding of how and what is the best for you, and then actually seeing it through, is going to be the most difficult, yet the most important, part of creating your new way of thinking. What matters most is how you are going to handle this for yourself. You have got to love yourself through it. People will judge you and what is worse, you will judge yourself. You may sit and worry and fret that there was something you could have done. You may "if only" yourself into a dark and dreary hole. You may lay all of the blame and fear, and hurt, right in your own lap until it breaks your legs. You may review all of the past and look for any hint of how you failed your loved one. You may convince yourself there was something you could have done to fix it all. It just isn't true. That decision was not yours. You had no say in what happened. How can you blame yourself for a decision where you had no chance to vote? We are back to fighting the dragon and one of the deadliest weapons this beast has is called: guilt. You have to get it off of you. You have to. Really, you Have To.

Letting go of the responsibility for what others think and do is the key. Staying true and loving to you, completely, is the iron clad collar which will hold that deadly dragon of emotion down. Your strength and belief in love will get you through just about everything. It has to start with you.

People suffer the death of loved ones every day, due to illness, accidents, etc. There are common reactions which occur during these times; shock, anger, loss of interest in work, disrupted sleep patterns, disrupted eating patterns, grief, helplessness, and feelings of abandonment, isolation, loneliness, shame and guilt. Suicide survivors are no exception, they go through all of these same feelings. However, they have greater difficulty with the process of grieving, by exhibiting their own list of symptoms: physical illness, depression, post traumatic stress syndrome, substance abuse and family breakdowns. Suicide survivors often feel that they are viewed more negatively by others and are typically viewed more negatively by themselves.

The Department of Health and Human Services, back in 1999, began lobbying for a method of therapy for suicide survivors that they called a: postvention. They determined suicide survivors often experienced less support, or were unaware of the support available to them. Combine this with the emotions of guilt and shame, the social stigma of suicide results in survivors feeling uncomfortable and awkward even with normal social support systems like family or friends. Many suicide survivors never look for help. Help is out there. Find it and take it. Below is a website which will help you. You don't have to heal alone. Remember, you are a bright and beautiful child of this miraculous Universe. You deserve to be happy, healthy and loved.

www.suicidology.com

When you go to this website, click on the "suicide loss survivors" tab. It will take you to a page with an alphabetical list, to find a support program in your area. If you do not live in the United States, please go to this website anyway, send them an email and let them guide you in finding the help you need.

Many people turn to psychics and mediums during this time, trying to connect with the loved one who has passed. If this is something you are considering, I want to give you a little caution to be careful about the medium you choose.

The best reference for any psychic or medium is word of mouth. If you don't know anyone who has seen a psychic or a medium, go to a reputable metaphysical store and talk to one of their readers. Most metaphysical stores will test their psychics before hiring. It is fine to ask the store staff any and all questions regarding the available readers.

The store staff will know each reader personally, and probably have had several readings with each of them. Let them guide you toward the psychic or medium who is best suited for you.

That doesn't mean there aren't fabulous readers out there who do not sit in a store. I have several really incredible psychic friends who work strictly from home. Like I said, word of mouth is the best resource.

I feel I need to give you a word of caution. If a psychic or medium mentions you have a curse, or there is some negative energy surrounding you which needs to be removed, *that* is a red flag. If the same reader tells you it will cost a large amount of money for the curse, or the energy, to be removed; run out of the place like your hair is on fire. Just because someone is psychic does not mean they are spiritual. Just like in any business, there are charlatans who are only out to make a buck. If a reader gives you a price for a reading, that should be the price. If you go over your allotted time the reader should warn you, to make sure you are okay paying the overage. It shouldn't cost extra to do mediumship, or to connect in a special way, in the middle of a reading.

All costs associated with the reading should be given to you upfront, by the scheduler or the reader.

A reader may tell you that you need some energy work done. It is probably true. A separate appointment, for an energy work session, should be made and the cost should be listed on an easy to understand menu of services. Energy work is valuable in healing emotional and physical wounds. Unexpected fees should not pop up in the middle of anything. If they do, end the reading, pay for the time you have taken, and be done. Love yourself enough to say, "enough".

You will feel the love from a good psychic or medium. They will want to help you. They will expect to be compensated. They will stay in their integrity. They may not be on time. They may not be easy to connect with. After all, they spend a lot of time in a realm where time means nothing.

PRELUDE TO THE OTHER SIDE
"WHAT DO YOU DO FOR A LIVING?"
GULP.

It's a question I always know is coming and always dread, like a trip to the dentist. Smiling people who meet me always ask me what I do. Their smiles will change when I give them the answer. A million questions fly across their minds and their confusion and discomfort shows like the lace on a too long slip.

I am a psychic. Yes, I am. It is not a comfortable job title in most parts of the south but it is what the Universe chose for me to do. I am also a medium. Yes, there is a difference between a psychic and a medium. Psychics can read your energy and connect to your guides and angels, or whoever they get their information from, and they can relay those messages back to you. A medium is someone who can communicate with the other side. They specialize in being able to talk to people who have passed on. I will tell you, every psychic I know gets different information and even if they have been trained, they will get that information in different ways. Everyone is different.

I know people perceive psychics and mediums in different ways. I know some people think being a psychic/medium is a magical and mystical way of life and that all psychics know everything, from the first moment they interact with another person. Well, I am here to tell you, it just doesn't work like that. I can't tell you when you are going to die. If I could, I wouldn't. I can't give you the lottery numbers. If I could, don't you think I wouldn't need to do readings? I would have given myself those precious numbers and skipped my dollar happily down to the gas station by now.

In truth, the information I get is given to me when, and where, and how the Universe, or Spirit or God, wants me to get it. I only get what is given, and it isn't up to me, or you.

I have been called a witch. I have been called a devil. I have been called an angel. In fact, I read for a delightfully, fabulous lady, in Kentucky, who is of the Pentecostal faith. She says, although many religions of the south look down upon people who are psychics, or who visit psychics, it isn't against her religion to talk to me. Because, she believes I am a prophet. It seems the Pentecostal people believe in seeking out prophets for guidance on their journey. I love her to pieces and laugh hard every time she says it. In all my years of looking at religions, I have yet to read about any prophet who colored their hair and drank bourbon.

I am not a prophet. I am not a mystical creature. I am just a person with sensitive wiring and that doesn't make me anymore special than having hazel eyes. It's genetic. I believe everyone is psychic. I believe we are all connected, on this earth or in the ether. We are all connected.

I have scads of clients who come to me on a regular basis. They use me as kind of a cosmic barometer, who gives them the upcoming weather report for their journey of life. They trust me, and I am grateful for them…and for the trust. It means everything.

I have also run across many people who are a little hostile about psychics. They preach we are all frauds, bilking money from gullible people. I don't have issue with those folks. I really don't. Some of the people who have given me the hardest time are the same ones that give money to well dressed television preachers in massive churches, and who live in fabulously decorated mansions. It's all in what you believe, so believe what you will; it is *your* belief system, right? Of course, right.

My own belief system regarding psychics has been a confusing one. Psychic ability was a hush, hush kind of thing in my family. Even though, my family was and is peppered with sensitives and healers. If you ask my mother (in front of anyone) if she believes in psychics, she will laugh and tell you, with big eyes, that she does not. But, she does, she really does. You can tell. She never, ever missed a Montel episode, with Sylvia Browne as a guest. Her eyes get big and she never makes a peep while the long nailed mystic drags out her low gravely predictions. She also never misses an episode of Medium or Ghost Whisperer. I feel pretty certain she probably hopes I don't remember her clutching my chubby, little hand as we made our way along the cracked and broken sidewalk up to the little house of "Rosie, the fortune teller". Rosie had a chicken in a little wooden box on her kitchen table. It was black and white. That has no relevance to this book, but the image has stuck in my head for forty years. I just thought I'd share it.

She believes. She can't tell me anything different…I know her history.

I have had a few other jobs in my past. I have been a professional singer, a hair stylist and nutrition services director for a large private non- profit organization. I have done readings professionally for about ten years. Two years ago, I quit my J-O-B and started reading full-time. I have landed in the most wonderful metaphysical bookstore, called the Phoenix and Dragon, in Atlanta, Georgia. If you are ever in town, please look it up and visit. You won't be disappointed.

I read for many people each week, and they all have different questions and stories. I love meeting all of them. Each person who sits with me is a precious gift, to me and to the world in general. And, I am glad to give them any help that I can.

Most people who come to me for readings have questions about their love life, real estate, or financial issues. Some folks call me to talk about their jobs and to see if they should leave or stay. Occasionally, I get people who want to connect with a deceased loved one and those times are always moving and good. I *love* love.

About five years ago, before I came to Georgia, I did a reading that changed my life. This reading set me on a path which, looking back, I am not sure I would have chosen to walk. It has been a magical, mind-blowing, conscious-altering journey. At the same time, it has kicked my behind to the floor. Regardless, it marked the beginning of a new life, new beliefs and a new purpose. In the next chapter, I will share with you the gift which was given to me. It was the cornerstone of what would become a new life and a new paradigm for me, a few years before I was going to need it.

THE GIFT

On the day of the reading, that changed it all, I was annoyed. I had gotten a call, the day before, from a woman who was promoting an event. She had offered me a chance to be one of the featured speakers. I was grateful for the opportunity and we had a nice chat. I was so stoked because this event was near Sedona Arizona and I had wanted to go there for a long time.

The next morning, when I checked my email, I noticed one which had been sent by her. I was happy to see confirmation of my workshop, but she would not be able to pay my airfare. I was disappointed; airfare to

Arizona was going to be a little pricey. As I continued to read, my spirits dropped even lower when I saw a request, asking if I would read for one of her friends, at no charge.

The event promoter went on to tell me, her friend was in a bad place in her life and she felt I was the one who could help her out. I agreed to the reading, and in my self-centered fear, I was feeling a little disrespected.

Little did I know, this reading would turn out to be a bigger gift to me than my small-mindedness could have ever imagined. I gave the promoter some time-slots I had open for appointments, and she scheduled the appointment for the next evening.

I went to work at the non-profit that day and by the time I got home, I was in full dread of the reading. I assumed this would be another reading of emotional questions about some cheating man, or an urgent request for predictions on a real estate transaction. Rolling my eyes and heaving a great sigh, I dialed the number. The phone only rang a couple of times before it was answered. On the other end of the phone line was a sobbing woman. I introduced myself and we exchanged greetings for just a couple of minutes. She began to cry even more and told me that she needed my help in connecting to her son who had committed suicide just three months before. To this point in my career, I had never been asked to connect with a suicide victim. My heart began pounding and my head started to reel as I prayed to be given the best information possible for this woman. All the while she was crying and begging me to try to connect with her son. I prayed, "Jesus, if you have ever given me the good stuff, it has to be now. I cannot hurt this woman anymore than she already hurts."

Without another moment passing, into my vision came a young man with shaggy, brown hair. Amazingly, he was being brought forward, almost carried, lifted under each of his arms, by two massive angels. I could barely speak from the sight of what I was being shown. It is not uncommon for me to see angels during readings, but these angels were like nothing I had ever seen. The first thing which amazed me was that they were huge, very tall and stately.

The second amazing thing was their color. They were crystal blue and sparkling, almost as if they were made from glittering glass. The angels were purposeful in their appearance. They were not there to look at me, talk to me, or even acknowledge me. It was as if they were some sort of guards, sent only to bring the young man forward, and to take him back. That is exactly what they did.

This shaggy-headed young man came in closer to me than I had ever experienced during a mediumship connection. He was brought so closely to me, that if he had been in human form, we would have bumped heads with a simple nod. The poor boy looked exhausted. His head hung down and dark sweeps of color surrounded his eyes. He didn't look like anyone I had ever seen on the other side. Most spirits, I connect to, are happy. They look wonderful and healthy. This young man looked sick. He looked weary. He gave me messages of apology, for his mother. He really hadn't meant to cause so much pain. He admitted he was thinking only of himself at the time. He explained how he had been sick in thought, his mind swirling and swirling for years.

The young man used very coarse words and graphic descriptions to describe how his mind had been working. The information came so quickly I didn't use much of a filter in the delivery. He relayed to his mother how his thoughts were like a clogged toilet that just kept swirling, and swirling, and the dirty mess of it was too much.

He began using drugs to escape the thoughts and had become addicted. He had gotten clean, at his family's request, and because he was going to be a father. Once he was clean, his thoughts began that terrible swirling again and he said he just couldn't take it any longer. He didn't want the battle of addiction and the non-acceptance of those he loved. But, he couldn't be tortured by his mind any longer.

He told me he was okay and even though he was tired, he was better than he had been in life. He also explained, he had a lot work to do, but if his mother needed him, all she needed to do was just ask. His energy was low but he explained how he could be in several places at one time. That concept was hard for his mother to imagine. I read for over an hour, my mind trying to process all of this new and confusing information, and give messages to his mother at the same time. When we ended the reading, his mother seemed to feel better about where her son was and how he was doing. Her energy seemed much calmer. She thanked me for the reading and told me she felt like she might be able to get some rest.

I, on the other hand, had some serious questions which would not leave. After all, I believed once you crossed to the other side it was all love and forgiveness, peace and tranquility. If that was the truth, then what were these angels who seemed almost like prison guards? Was there really the harsh punishments and judgments I had been warned about in my youth? I had seen him brought forward by angels and they were not dark or frightening. They seemed to come from the light of the Holy Spirit. That was not an indication of any purgatory or hell. The young man, however, was tired and exhausted. He didn't seem happy or rejuvenated or any of the things I had seen from other souls once they had crossed to the other side. I was baffled and plenty confused. Since, I never question the information Spirit gives me during readings, I set the whole confusing experience aside in my mind for the rest of the night and well into the next day.

When I finally went into meditation, late the next day, I asked for any messages from my guides and angels. I received a small, almost greeting card like message. "Be brave like the lion and gentle like the lamb." I waited for more but nothing more came. I was confused; it was definitely not a typical message from my usual long-talking guides. I closed my eyes again, focused on my question and asked why their message was so short. The response I received was, "It is not the answer you truly seek." As usual, my guides were right. It wasn't what was on my mind. I had been fighting the urge to analyze what I had seen in the reading. I didn't want to bring it up, or to question it. And, honestly, I wasn't really sure I wanted to know the answers. That is some pretty deep stuff and I really wasn't sure I was ready for it. Then the understanding dawned on me. If I had not been ready, my guides would not have been so eager to share the information. So, I took a deep breath and asked the one question which was the most perplexing, "What were those angels?"

The message I was given is this:
"You *are correct in that they are guardians or sentries. They are charged with guarding the souls that come to them for healing. You are incorrect in your thinking of this soul's captivity. This is a situation of protection of the soul energy. There is accountability for the soul energy, but not as you have imagined. Each soul energy must be responsible for the seeing, the feeling, and*

the aiding in the repair of the deficit of energy they have left, in ending their life. The soul energy must see the grief they have caused and must feel the grief that their loved ones are feeling. As situations arise, it is in the soul energy's power to be of assistance. During these times, the soul energy must aid to repair the situation, as it is brought before them. It is this accountability. It is all in the realm that you call Heaven. They are in the care and the love of the Father for all time.

The etheric beings you name angels are responsible for bringing this young man forward during your connection to help him repair the instances of deficit he had left for his mother. They accompanied him and aided the soul energy because his own energy was not strong enough for him to come through on his own. And, it was not strong enough to get him back to the other side, without assistance."

I was then shown a place where suicide victims go, once they cross. It was bright, and white, and clean. The energy of the structures was sparkling as if painted with crystal. It made me think of a hospital. My guides made me understand the majority of people who take their own life are spiritually ill. They have lost hope and light, and are in need of a great deal of love. This place, which seemed like a hospital, was where they went. Special angels were there to surround them with love and healing. They could stay as long as they needed, before going on to continue their soul's journey in another realm. Some souls stay and participate in the healing of others. Some stay for a very long time. There seemed to be no time table in this place. It was very quiet and peaceful, with soft pink love energy everywhere. I could see angels and other spirit energies surrounding those who needed healing. There wasn't any judgment. There wasn't any pressure. There was only love and acceptance. There was so much kindness and peaceful support.

These etheric beings were helping those souls in the forgiveness and the acceptance of themselves, and to guide them as they worked through their lessons. There was no hell fire. There was no eternal damnation. There was plenty of good, old, tough-love, and plenty of it … lots of unconditional, never-ending, powerful and peaceful love. It was after receiving this information that I began to say "It's all about the love".

Susan Rushing

TRIPTIK FROM THE UNIVERSE

When the Universe gives you a mission, you better take it my friend. When you are called, there is no time to wallow in your self-doubt or fear. No way. The first time an offer is made and you ignore it, it doesn't mean the mission goes away. Oh no. The mission is still yours. The purpose is yours completely. When you ignore the Universe, it thinks you have a hearing problem. So, when you ignore that first pleasant whisper in your ear, the Universe adjusts. Maybe the next time, you will get a much less subtle and more disturbing hint. If you ignore that, the next time the Universe is going to pop you with a cosmic wet towel, right in the locker room of life. Just answer the call the first time. Really, it's just better for everyone.

That first experience of connecting with suicide, from the other side, was like the Universe handing me a ticket to walk down a path I didn't really want to walk. Even though those kinds of readings seemed to pop up once or twice a month, I didn't take it to heart. I continued on for a couple of years, reading part-time, with suicide readings popping up frequently. When my other psychic friends told me I needed to write about it, or read full time, I didn't do it. I remember saying to one of my most adamant friends, "Who is going to want to listen to me, really? I mean, who am I to be getting this kind of information? Who is going to believe me? I am just a fat, red head living in Kentucky. Do I really want to be known as "the suicide medium?"

Finally I wrote an article about what I had seen. It was published in an online magazine. I did several internet radio interviews and soon my part-time appointment book was filled with people who wanted to connect with the other side. My psychic friends were cheering me on, for putting this knowledge out into the world. But, at the same time, they chastised me for not following my path completely by reading full-time. Down inside, I knew they were right. So, I went into meditation to make a deal with the Universe and my Cosmic Posse. The deal was that I would quit my full time job if the Universe provided me with no less than 5 readings per week for 5 weeks. That would be enough money to equal my pay check and to make ends meet.

I set the intention, and within two days I had five readings lined up for the week. In two weeks, I couldn't keep up with the demand for readings every evening. It seemed like as soon as I did one reading, another person would call for an appointment. I was amazed and flabbergasted and also secretly afraid the Universe was going to follow through, and I would have to quit my job at the private non-profit and give up the steady paycheck.

By week five, I had more readings on my appointment book than I had originally asked. But, because I let fear override me, I allowed myself to believe the rush of appointments would never last. Even though this had happened, just as I had asked, I told myself there was no promise the readings would continue to be steady. I was so worried that I wouldn't be able to pay the bills, I freaked out and I didn't hold up my end of the deal. I kept my job for another year and kept reading part-time.

So, the Universe did what it always does when you don't hold up your end of the bargain. It hit me where I lived. It hit me in the heart.

Okay, it hit me in the heart, opened my mind, and kicked me in the behind…all at the same time. It all started with a single phone call that would change my life and the world as I knew it. Anyway, I finally got the message, took the hint, read the memo…it went a little something like this:

Dear Susan,

Here is your map. Here is your ticket. Here is the plan. Speak the love. You will be provided for.

Love, Spirit

P.S. Wear a helmet.

Actually, it would have been a lot nicer to get a verified message from the Universe, like that. The Universe is sneaky. I fully believe the "powers that be" knew they were going to have to trick me a little, to get what they needed out of me. The whole thing came out of the blue. As I have said before, gifts come when you least expect them. This gift was no exception.

I speak at events. I don't do it a lot, but I always love it when I do. I love people and I love to hear their stories and I love to hug their necks. Everyone has an interesting tale to tell. If you sit long enough with folks, you will find they can entertain and educate you just by telling you what they have been through. I have always believed there is purpose in every connection. Sometimes, it might be something negative you need to learn about. Most of the time, it is just a loving message delivered in an entertaining way. I love that.

I spoke at a conference, in Atlanta, a few years ago and met some wonderful people there. During my presentation, I mentioned I was in need of being able to add audio files, of grounding exercises, to my website. At the end of the session, a woman approached me with a business card that read "ideaLand". She told me her partner could help me put the audio files on my website. In the back of the room was a short, dark haired girl, wearing a newsboy hat turned backwards. She was nodding at me and waived a little. I was grateful to find someone who knew what I was talking about and I took the card gladly.

A couple of months went by before I got around to calling. I was immediately connected to Sondra, the web designer. She told me she could help me with my website and, luckily, they could give me a discount. All I needed was to give her some ideas and colors to work with and she would work up some different designs. I was jumping around the room, I was so excited. I was actually going to have a real, professionally designed site. Ice that cake with a discount and I was in absolute bliss. The Universe had delivered, again. Hooray! Even though I was so excited, there was an odd energy about that call. It felt a little dangerous and I couldn't tell if it was the change I was feeling or if I was worried about spending the money.

When I finally connected with Sondra again, a couple of months later, it was on a social network. You know the one, I don't want to say the name out loud but it rhymes with Bacefook. We spoke briefly about the website and then Sondra also said she had read my suicide article, and she liked it. She told me her grandfather had committed suicide. She seemed to be a little sad and confused about his passing. I asked her if she wanted to talk and see if we could connect to him. She said "yes." She typed in her number; I picked up the phone and dialed it. Sondra answered in the first couple of rings and we immediately began the reading.

I called in my guides and angels, along with Sondra's guides and angels to ask for help in assisting in the connection. I was immediately connected to a man who was short and had dark hair. He was there with two beautiful crystalline angels, as I had seen in other readings. However, these angels were of a different color. Sondra's grandfather's angels were a lovely shade of green. I also noticed he was wearing a grey sweater vest. The vest was thick and knobby looking, like it had been hand knitted. I told Sondra about the vest and she didn't think it was anything that he would have worn. She told me he had emphysema and had suffered with it so badly that he killed himself. I wondered if the vest was a representation of his illness. Perhaps, he was still working through it and wore it like a garment.

Through the conversation he stayed present but offered no words. His mouth seemed to be sealed shut. He finally hung his head and moved out of connection. I did feel a great amount of love from him toward Sondra. There was an odd sadness about this man, almost like he was disappointed in himself. I reassured

Sondra that her grandfather was okay and how I had seen him with angels. He was on the other side and was healing. When the reading was over, I expected Sondra to hang up quickly. I mean, that's what usually happens at the end of a reading, people get the information they need, and then end the call. This time was different. She didn't end the call and we continued talking for a couple of hours.

Over the course of the next few weeks, Sondra and I developed a great friendship with one another. We talked every evening when I got home from work, discussing everything from music to angels, to religion, to extra terrestrials. I loved talking with a smart, not only like-minded, but open-minded person. I was thrilled to be able to discuss all of the things I had been shown or had seen, without judgment, correction, or debate. She seemed to be content with my views and didn't hesitate to tell me her own. I am grateful for these calls. During this time, I was able to really think deeply and freely about what I had been shown during those readings and how it related to the world. It gave me a steady foundation in my belief…of me. That, ladies and gentlemen is priceless.

GRANDFATHER REVISITS

One evening, while Sondra and I were talking, her grandfather came to me, out of the blue. Accompanying him were the same two shiny green angels. But, this time, that thick gray vest was undone and hanging open. He said to me, "I am finally taking off this vest. I am ready to talk." I told Sondra he was with us and was ready to say what he needed to say. As he spoke to me, I relayed to Sondra what he was saying. In my mind's eye, I watched him begin to shed the vest.

He moved slowly and it seemed the vest was very old and heavy. When he had completely removed it he began speaking.

"Tell Sondra I love her and I love them all. I never stopped loving any of them. Tell her Grandmother that I always loved her. I always thought she was the most beautiful girl in the world. I never believed I was good enough for her. Even after we were married, I never believed it. She was shiny, like a diamond. She *was* a diamond. I never felt good enough for a diamond. I had to go out and find glass because that was what I was suited for. I was never, ever good enough for someone like Opal, but I always loved her best. She was just too good for me. That's all."

After having finished speaking his heart, he turned toward the big green angels and faded back from connection. The energy felt a little sad and content at the same time. I am sure I was feeling my own sadness at this man who had loved a woman but could not love himself. Once out of my view, I said a silent gratitude that he had finally gotten to take off that terrible vest.

It was during his speech I realized the sweater vest was not related to his lung illness, at all. That sweater vest was the guilt he was packing around.

It laid on him and threatened to smother him. The angels who brought him forward were there to help him remove the guilt from his heart. He wasn't ready to let it go during that first phone call, or perhaps he wasn't strong enough at the time of his first reading. He had been ready this time, and he was coming through to do what he needed to do, whether we called him or not. It was important. It had to be done. I was glad to be allowed to help.

Sondra did tell her mother about the reading and her mother recanted the message to Opal. Whether Opal believed it or not, I don't know. I do know she will believe it when she sees him again. As I hung up the phone, I felt the energy shift. I wasn't sure why, but after that reading, a pattern began to emerge during these readings. It tied a great many of my spiritual teachings together. I have been working with energy since I was a small child. I recognized energy healing and that's what was going on. Of course it was, we are all energetic beings, how else could we be healed? My mind buzzed with excitement. I was onto something and it was a big something.

It was during, and after, this reading I began paying attention to the subtle differences and consistencies in the spirits who came through. I began noticing how the angels which appeared with each spirit came through in different colors. Those colors seemed to coordinate with chakra colors which were associated with the issue each spirit was dealing with at the moment. Now, let me just say right here, if you don't know what a chakra is, just hang on. We are going to talk about it, later. I promise.

For instance, in the first reading, the angels were a crystal blue. The color blue is the color associated with the fifth or throat chakra. The young man needed to speak his truth to tell his mother the real reason that he had to take his life. He needed to use the throat chakra energy to do that. The angels who accompanied him, vibrated at that color frequency to support him in this mission. Those angels were there to bring the young man forward and to assist him in getting back, but they were also his support team in another very important way. They were helping him to heal by supporting the energy which he needed to speak his truth. It is beautiful, how it works.

I talked in depth about all of this with Sondra and didn't leave out a detail. She didn't seem shocked. She didn't change the subject. She didn't get uncomfortable and the best part was that she didn't think I was crazy.

She believed me and listened to every story and every thought as if we were talking about the news or sharing thoughts on a movie. It felt like I was okay in this new way of thinking about the other side. She made me feel a little more like normal. Talking about what I had been experiencing was making even the most "out there" of my psychic friends raise their eyebrows. Their reactions began making me question what I was being shown. Sondra listened and gave me feedback and food for thought. Because I was able to discuss and verbalize these things, I felt more confident to look deeper into each reading. I came to understand how there really was a pattern. In the next chapter, I want to share a few of those readings with you, just so you can see the pattern too.

Susan Rushing

ENCOUNTERING SOULS
THE READINGS

In this section, I want to share some of the amazing suicide readings I have experienced. I am including seven stories, just like in the bible. Except here, there are no wars. There are no buildings collapsing. There are only souls who share their stories of struggle and their stories of love and healing. I hope these beautiful folks will inspire you and assist you in understanding what happens on the other side when suicide is involved.

I also hope this information might give you some peace in knowing when "they" say the Lord is forgiving, it is truly, one of the only times "they" speak the pure unaltered truth.

Forgiveness is love and love is the only thing that is real. Love will hold no anger. Love will turn away fear. Love will set a spirit free, and it will, indeed conquer all. I hope you will see this for yourself and begin your own process of making peace and forgiveness with yourself, and with everyone else in your life both on earth and on the other side.

I want to say a special thank you to all of the people, living and passed on, who have sat with me and shared their stories and pain, love and healing. I am grateful and humbled that you have entrusted me with these special energies. I love you all.

To my dear readers; the following readings are true. Please understand the names and sometimes gender, mentioned in the recanting of these readings, have been altered. I am all about confidentiality for my clients. And, if I am being completely honest; even though I never forget an energy, I have a lousy memory for names.

Ginny

The first reading I would like to share with you is one of my very favorites. Sometimes, talking with the dead can be like playing charades in a snowstorm. This reading was not like that. It was the clearest and happiest reading I have ever had the pleasure of doing.

I have to tell you, the woman who came through in this reading did not commit suicide. Her name was Ginny, and she died of lung cancer. I am including her in this book because Ginny is honestly my most favorite reading, ever. She also gave me the most incredible and helpful bits of information I have ever received during a reading. I want to share these with you because; I feel they will help you understand how spirit energy works. Ginny gave me the best analogy of what it is like to be in spirit. I think it helps people wrap their heads around how their loved ones can be doing all of the things they need to be doing on the other side and still be with us on this plane. I know that sounds a little confusing, but just bear with me, Ginny is going to shed some light, in her most cosmically fabulous way.

I received a phone call for a reading one afternoon. I was surprised to find myself on the speakerphone, with five sisters who were on a road trip. These five women were Ginny's daughters. All five sisters were in one car, driving from Ohio to Mississippi. The girls had their mother's ashes in the car with them and they were sprinkling them on every casino from Ohio to Mississippi, because spending time in a casino was what Ginny loved to do best. That old girl just loved to play the slot machines. Ginny raised five fun loving daughters who wanted to honor their mother in the shiniest way possible. On their way through the south, the girls called to ask me if it would be possible to connect with their mother, just to be sure they were doing the right thing.

The energy of those five fabulosities was just pure love and laughter. I couldn't help smiling, as I began to acclimate myself to their energies. I greeted each and everyone on speaker phone and assured those ladies I would do what I could to connect with their mother.

I called in my guides and angels, and I called in the guides and angels of each one of the five sisters. As I connected, a big smile involuntarily ran across my lips and immediately a small glamour queen came through to me with such playful energy, it made me laugh out loud. I mentioned to the girls that their mother was a funny woman. They all laughed and agreed wholeheartedly. It seems that Ginny was quite a character in this lifetime, and crossing over hadn't changed that one little bit.

She had been a hair stylist who owned and operated a beauty shop, in the garage of her house. In Ginny's own flamboyant, funny, and very quick-witted style, she gave me information about, and for, each of her daughters. She expressed her big love and stayed with us for close to an hour. She told each of her girls that she was with them every day and told us that she was working and playing in the realm we called "Heaven". When one of the girls took issue with Ginny's ability to be with all five girls and still be on the other side at the same time, Ginny finally got a little serious and proceeded to give me this fabulous analogy:

Imagine that you are a container of cottage cheese. (I know it may be difficult to think of yourself as a container of cottage cheese. Believe me; it was even harder for me. I can't stand cottage cheese. I have actually thought of changing the story a little from cottage cheese to a container of whipped topping. That is certainly more appealing. I mean, who doesn't love whipped topping? But, my job is to give the information straight as I get it. So, we stick with cottage cheese.)

The outside plastic cup with the writing on it represents your body. Inside the plastic cup is the cottage cheese. The cottage cheese represents your soul.

When a person's body dies, the lid can be taken off of the cottage cheese container, and now the cottage cheese can come out. Now, as we said before, the cottage cheese is a direct representation of your spirit energy. We all know from science class, energy cannot be destroyed, but it can be manipulated. So, a scoop of that cottage cheese can be put on a plate in Georgia, a scoop can be put on a plate in Ohio, a scoop in California, a scoop in Canada, a scoop in France, and one can be placed on a plate in Heaven. It is still the same cottage cheese; it can just be in lots of different places at the same time, because it can be divided.

Ginny says that we get so hung up on our containers that we can't understand how we work without one. Energy can be divided to do what it needs to do. It is still the same energy at full potential. It can just be everywhere and anywhere.

That moment was really big for me. I have always believed we are the same energy as our creator. I believe we all share the same cosmic DNA of big love.

It is said that our creator can be everywhere, at all times. If we are made from that same energy, it stands to reason we can be everywhere, at all times, too…without our containers.

After 45 minutes of terrific information peppered with bursts of laughter, Ginny began to pull back a little, she told us she needed to go because she was having cocktails with Elvis and she didn't want to be late. Her daughters laughed heartily and told me Ginny was an Elvis junkie from as far back as anyone of them could remember. I wasn't surprised.

As I closed the reading, I thanked Ginny for coming through and for all she had imparted and as I closed connection, I expressed a silent gratitude to Ginny for all of her glitteriness, and for giving me the correct tools to help people on this side understand life on the other. That ball of cosmic clarity named Ginny was a blessing and a gift to many people, and I was now added to that list. I am grateful for Ginny.

You see, this is just another reason why, when we find a good hair stylist, we should stay with her as long as we can.

Rebecca

One of the things I am most moved by, while doing readings, is how people on the other side want to connect and make peace for their loved ones. This next story is a good example of this. The client was coming in for a reading about her professional life and without hesitation the spirit of a lovely woman named Rebecca took the opportunity to make herself known, and didn't give up until she had given the loving energy that she needed to give to her long time friend.

I was introduced to the spirit of Rebecca through her friend, Maggie. Maggie came into the shop for a 30 minute reading. She hadn't asked for mediumship when she made the appointment. Needless to say, I wasn't ready for the story which was about to unfold before me. When Maggie sat down and I connected to her guides and angels, I immediately began to feel dizzy and queasy. I didn't have an image of anyone coming through in my mind's eye, so I asked Maggie if she had been having any dizzy spells. She told me she hadn't been dizzy at all. Confused, I tried to blow it off, wondering if my sugar level might be off. Despite the dizziness, I continued the reading.

Maggie had a slew of questions regarding her budding business. I gave her answers as best I could, but I couldn't shake the dizziness and the almost overwhelming stomach pain.

Midway through the reading I asked Maggie if she knew of anyone on the other side who might have suffered dizziness or nausea when they passed. I could tell by the look on her face that those symptoms weren't ringing any bells. I took another deep breath and went on with the reading.

With only a few minutes left of our 30 minute reading, finally the slender face of a middle aged woman faded in and out of my mind. I stopped Maggie's questions and began describing the woman and all of her lovely, delicate features to Maggie. As I spoke, Maggie's eyes grew wide and filled with tears. She leaned her face into her hands and began to cry. She looked up and grabbed a Kleenex and told me I was describing her long-time friend; Rebecca. Once Maggie had identified and acknowledged Rebecca, this lovely, gentle spirit moved forward into clearer view.

The energy of Rebecca was like a painting in pastel watercolor. The colors of her swirled about, in peach, pink and turquoise blue. And, as she began to take form, I could see she was sensitive, gentle and beautiful. Even though, she was just the slightest bit careworn. Rebecca was escorted by two beautiful golden angels, who glistened and shone like the sun. Rebecca asked me to reassure Maggie that she was alright; she had made it to the other side without any difficulty.

Rebecca told us she was in a healing place. She was happy and working. She apologized to Maggie for hurting her. Rebecca relayed to us how she had begun to die in her heart, long before her body would give out. When her heart began to die, she began to become desensitized to the outside world. She told us she didn't mean to cause so much confusion for others. As her life was, at the time of her suicide, Rebecca just couldn't manage to see anything further than her own overwhelming situation. As she began to give me images of her story, Maggie chimed in and told me the story as she knew it. My heart ached for this lovely, gentle and sensitive woman and all that she had to endure during her time here on earth.

Rebecca and her husband were a happy couple. They met and married in their late thirties, and immediately set out to have a baby. It wasn't long before they got the wonderful news that they were expecting. It was a boy. That boy was their joy and passion. He was their only child. Their family and their lives were perfect for 17 years, until one night their son was involved in a fatal car accident. Rebecca and her husband were overcome with grief and their once happy lifestyle turned into a nightmare. Rebecca and her husband clung tightly to one another for many years to get through the grief of losing their only child.

Many years later, Rebecca's husband was diagnosed with lung cancer. The cancer grew rapidly and within a few short months, Rebecca's husband joined their son on the other side. The loss was too immense for Rebecca. She felt so helpless. She felt so hopeless. She felt so alone. She couldn't stand the pain. She didn't want to be in this life without the two people who meant everything to her. Rebecca tried, for awhile, but it seemed as if she just couldn't find her power any longer. She couldn't find a reason to be here. Rebecca had saved up the prescriptions of pills the doctor had given her to help her sleep. And, one night she took them all at the same time.

Rebecca apologized several times to Maggie, and assured her that she had been the best friend she had ever had. Rebecca explained how her joy had been taken, her power was gone and she couldn't bear this world any longer. Maggie cried a lot in that reading, but she did her best to understand. Rebecca had been a very sensitive and emotional person in life, and it seemed this world was just too much for her to survive in alone. Feeling helpless and powerless, she did the only thing she could think of, and that was to try and find the two people who made her life on earth complete.

When I had a moment to review this reading, one of the first things that stood out in my mind was the color of those two angels. They were brilliant, sun-shine, gold and by far the brightest angels I had ever seen. The color yellow is the same vibration of the third chakra, also called the solar plexus chakra. The third chakra is known as the power center. Those golden angels were giving Rebecca the energy she needed to find her power again. They were supporting her in the way she needed to be able to talk to her friend in a powerful and meaningful way. They were vibrating at the level, the precise level, required to help her heal. They were supporting her energetically. Strong, supportive, and working completely on their purpose, these angels are never distracted from what they are there to do.

I see these kinds of angels in every suicide reading I do, and I am always in awe of these etheric beings.

Abigail

I have read for so many teen suicides and every one breaks my heart. I understand the Universe has reasons for everything, but I cannot get past the untapped potential of these sensitive souls.

Abigail was just 16 when she took her own life. She was artistic, charming, athletic and beautiful. I know it sounds perfect, but it wasn't for Abigail.

High accountability and impeccable standards were an everyday routine in this young lady's house. When she came forward, during a reading with her father, I knew by the two large orange angels, there were going to be some touchy subjects to talk about. At first, I only could see an image of her and the angels. The way she presented herself was almost with her back to me, looking over her shoulder. I could tell she didn't want to talk. She stood there with her arms folded across her chest and her lips closed tightly, it didn't take a psychic to decipher that particular body language.

I could only give a description of her to her father. He began tearing up and asking questions. Most were questions of her purpose and why had she done what she had done. I looked to Abigail for answers. She stood looking at me, mouth closed, arms crossed. She was definitely not talking. This was going to be a tough one.

I figured, if I was going to get any information, I was going to have to look to those angels for answers. Suicide angels never talk. As I have said, in a previous portion of this book, they don't even look at me. So, this time, I had to look at them. I had to analyze their energy and try to understand Abigail from it.

I could see the angels were orange. Orange is related to the second or sacral chakra. I know the sacral chakra houses creativity. Ok...it was a small bone, but a bone nonetheless.

I told Abigail's dad I was sensing his daughter was a creative girl. He agreed, and went on about how talented she was in many things. He told me about beautiful paintings, drawings and poetry that had come from his only daughter. He also mentioned Abigail had given up some of her art because she was getting into sports, at the urging of her parents. They wanted her to be as well-rounded as she could be.

I looked back at Abigail. She was still there, arms folded, mouth still closed. So, I had to go back to the angels.

Sacral Chakra...also houses issues with mother

relationship and with children. Abigail was just 16; I didn't feel there were any children.

Stepping out on a limb, I told Dad I felt there might be some issues with Mom. Once I said that out loud, an amazing thing happened. Abigail uncrossed her arms and turned to face me. I was on to something. Then something incredible and mind blowing happened. Those two orange angels began to change. Colors began to swirl and spin and didn't settle down until both angels were a mixture of orange and yellow.

This was the first time I had ever seen bi-colored angels. This new vision was surprising and distracting. I had a great deal of trouble concentrating. Yellow and Orange, second and third chakras: creativity, sexuality, mother relationship, power. There was something, with which we could work.

Taking the new information into consideration, I went further out on that limb and said I felt Abigail's power had been taken, frequently, by her mother. I was worried, but I wasn't surprised, when her father began to passionately defend his wife. Just when I began thinking I had seriously overstepped a boundary and was in for a verbal smack down, he began to soften. He agreed that Abigail's mother was controlling, but she had only been that way to make Abigail the best she could be. A moment later, he began blaming himself for taking Abigail's power too. At that, he began to cry. When Abigail's Dad began to cry, Abigail began to speak.

Abigail really was an artistic girl. She showed me how much she loved color, and how she appreciated art in all forms. She spoke of her great love for her brother, and how she felt terrible about hurting him. She showed me so many practical jokes that she and her brother played on one another, almost daily. Abigail told me her brother was smart and quick-thinking, and she was watching over him all the time.

She said her biggest regret was that she had left everyone so upset. She didn't want anyone to be upset. She wanted it to all go back to the way it was, only without her. She just needed to be out of the pressure. The recent push for her to put down her art and to move toward athletics was stressful. That stress combined with the stress from schoolwork and extracurricular activities was exhausting. Abigail excelled at everything. She knew success meant approval and approval meant love. She worked hard for her parents' approval, but there was something about Abigail she knew her parents would never approve of. Abigail had a best friend, and her name was Sara. Where there was one you would always see the other. Abigail loved Sara, and Sara loved Abigail. Rumors of their relationship had started to circulate around school. When Sara's mother talked to Abigail's mother about her concern over the relationship, Abigail's mother strongly suggested to Abigail that she find another best friend. She ended the friendship, as her mother requested. It was painful for both girls.

Abigail told me, even though ending her friendship with Sara was hard, she knew that if it wasn't Sara, there would be another girl, in another time, and it wouldn't ever be okay. It was one thing she couldn't change. It was one thing she was sure her parents wouldn't approve of and she couldn't live without their love.

Abigail asked me not to relay to her father of her sexuality. So, I didn't. I just told him Abigail was under a great deal of pressure and was unable to express herself in the way that she needed. She was just too sensitive for this world.

As I closed the reading and thanked Abigail for coming forward, she asked me to tell her father to look for a feather from her. When I told her father, his eyes grew large and he commented he had found a huge feather in the floor of his car that very morning.

Reflecting on this reading was a hard one for me. Young people are so filled with promise and potential. As I looked back, at Abigail's angels, I saw reflected all of the issues we talked about.

Those orange and yellow angels represented the sacral chakra, which holds our issues with sexuality and romantic relationships, and the solar plexus chakra that holds our personal power. Abigail's power had been taken in all aspects of her life, but the one thing she knew she could never change was in the sacral chakra.

I have one more story, with this theme, to write about in this book. But, I have read for many souls with stories just like it.

Statistics show that gay and lesbian teens are five times more likely to commit suicide then their heterosexual counterparts.

That's not okay.

Before I get on my soapbox, let me tell you about Martin.

Martin

As I move into Martin's reading, I want to preface the story with a note of advice to anyone seeking a reading or advice from a psychic or a medium. If a psychic gives you something that makes sense to you, tell them. When you continually deflect information, just because you aren't getting the actual name with correct spelling as it appeared on a birth certificate, you will short yourself out of a decent reading. You don't have to tell the whole story, just a simple nod of the head will do.

What happens is the reader will begin to second guess the information which he or she is being given, and then their analytical mind will come in and shut the reading down. You will see a prime example of this in my story of Martin. By the time Martin came through, I was so over his mother that really only a soul as radiantly fabulous as Martin could get me through it.

Martin's mom came in for a reading and didn't want to tell me a damned thing. She sat there with her arms folded and legs crossed and a blank expression on her face. When I connected to her energy, I was immediately foggy headed and nauseated. By this point, I had gotten accustomed to feeling this and knew exactly what I was picking up.

I told her I was dizzy and nauseated. I told her I felt like someone was coming through who had either been on morphine in their last days or had taken some heavy duty medication right before passing. I looked at her, and she shook her head. It was an unmistakable sensation, and her response left me a little confused.

So, I asked my guides if they could get a gender or relationship. I immediately got an M name (now I will tell you right here, I often get a solid first initial or a "sounds like" name, but a pure, straight out name…is a rarity for me.)

My guides also let me know the relationship was family, but the energy was more like friendship between the woman and the spirit.

I told the woman I was getting an M name and it felt like family, but there was a strong friendship bond between the two of them.

The woman shook her head again.

The information I was getting was pretty clear. I began wondering if this woman had someone else in mind to connect to, and was disregarding anyone else.

I asked my guides for more information. I got that this person was a male and had a younger sister and an older brother. The younger sister, he was close to. The older brother made fun of him. I relayed the information to the woman. Again, she shook her head.

At this point, I was beginning to think I was not getting good information, and I tried to close out the reading. Clearly frustrated with me, Martin's mother shouted, "Okay! I want to know about my son, Martin!"

Well, now I was really confused. My guides were giving me information about a close personal family member coming through, who was male, had a brother and a sister, and had a first name that began with an "M". None of that information was clicking with her? At this point, I couldn't understand how it didn't. I had a young man who wanted to communicate, and even though the information he was giving me sounded exactly like what his mother was telling me, she was clearly denying it could have been him. I was frustrated, beyond belief. Maybe, her son, Martin was still alive.

Going on the information I had gotten so far, and a little tickle in the back of my head, I asked her if her son was still here on the earth plane.

"No! He killed himself six months ago!" she shouted at me.

And, with that, in came Martin with two of the

craziest angels I had ever seen. Martin's angels were purple and blue, with flashes of orange and red, and one big dose of yellow. They were like a Technicolor feast for the eyes. Because of the psychic taffy pull I had just been through with Martin's mother, I had started to feel a little put off by her and her harshness. But, I have to say, with the sight of Martin and his multi-colored angels; it was very hard to stay engaged with Martin's mother. Martin was far more interesting than anything else in the room.

Martin was a beautiful boy, with black wavy hair and large blue eyes. I knew the minute I saw him, he had been a psychic child and his empathic ability was part of his downfall. Martin told me his parents had split up for a while. Everyone thought he was devastated by it, but his parents break-up didn't bother him. He loved his mother. She loved him and accepted him and showered him with all of the wonderful things he loved. She was his best friend, according to Martin. Martin was happy his mother was finally doing the things she loved to do, and finally being happy.

Martin's father wasn't so terrific in Martin's eyes. He always ridiculed him and made him feel less than worthy. He called Martin weak and a sissy, and was often overbearing and demanding. Martin told me he was trying to work through forgiveness for his father and to accept him in love. And, hopefully the energy of it would heal his father in some way.

Martin told me he was closest to his little sister and told me he watched her every day. He told me how he hated to leave her and it was one of his biggest regrets. He told me she was very athletic and he was going to do his best to send energy for the best outcomes for her, in her education. He told me she was a great nurturer and would be an excellent teacher and molder of people. He told me it was his plan to do everything he could, from the other side, to help her along. His energy shone brightly as he spoke. I could sense his excitement and pride of purpose in helping his little sister walk her path.

Martin's energy shifted a bit and he hung his head as he spoke of his older brother. Martin loved his brother, but it was a hard love. Martin told me his brother was also an athlete and was a hard teaser, calling Martin every derogatory term for being gay he could imagine. Martin loved his brother, and he knew his brother loved him back. He understood his brother was ribbing him in order to toughen him up. He knew his brother didn't want to think that Martin was gay, which made it even harder for him. Martin had known for as long as he could remember that he was gay. Martin told me he loved and forgave his brother and none of that mattered anymore.

I asked Martin if that was the reason for taking his own life. Martin shook his head and showed me that he had been talking to another young man, on the internet, for a few months. The two had met and connected a few times, and Martin believed they were getting closer. He held his secret close to his chest, never telling anyone that he had fallen in love for the first time. Who could he tell?

His mother was off doing her own thing. His father was already disapproving of him. His sister and brother made fun of him for being effeminate. It would have to remain a happy secret. Everything was fine; he didn't need to tell anyone.

However, when Martin's boyfriend suddenly ended the relationship, he was devastated. He grew sullen and depressed, and once again had no one to talk with about it.

Feeling like he was going to explode with emotion, Martin combed through every medicine cabinet he could find until he had dozens of muscle relaxers and pain killers. One afternoon when no one was home, he swallowed every one of them just as he had swallowed his truth for most of his life.

Martin was a young, psychically gifted, artistic, sensitive, gay man. His angels wore the colors of his secrets which needed to be revealed:

Purple for his repressed psychic ability and his third eye chakra.

Blue for his inability to speak his truth and his throat chakra.

Green for his broken heart and his heart chakra.

Yellow for his power being taken, by having to lie about his life and the constant pressure and teasing from others, and his solar plexus chakra.

Orange for his creativity, sexuality, mother issues and his sacral chakra.

Red for his inability to ground himself, and for the lack of acceptance from his father and his root chakra.

The world lost a treasure on the day Martin took his life. It is the same as Abigail and so many other gay and lesbian teens, or really any teen for that matter. Bright, talented and so full of potential, but the narrow-mindedness and short-sightedness of people on this planet, forced on young malleable and sensitive minds, can be overwhelming and make it seem like there is nowhere to turn. Combine that with bullies, insensitive school districts, news stations and social networks which bombard young people with anti-gay messages and you have a cocktail for destruction.

It hurts my heart to know these lovely souls felt like they had nothing left to give, or to live for, when the Universe was waiting for them to make it a better place. Love the children, no matter what.

Listen, just a little heads up…a gay child who is treated well and accepted, without ridicule or without judgment, will love you and take care of you and hold you up on a pedestal.

Don't lose your children because they are different. You have been entrusted with something precious, and they are precious to us all, no matter what anyone else thinks.

Sheila

It has taken me a full year to complete this book. Most of it was written in three months. A couple of pieces were missing, and I couldn't get past them. There was just something more I had not been given, and so, I had to wait. One of the last pieces of this book came in with a charming young woman named Bethany.

Bethany came to me surrounded by nervous energy. I mean, really, you could have plugged a lamp into her she was so charged. We had a great connection and I enjoyed her spirit. My time with her was pleasant and we got a great deal of information during the reading, regarding her very gifted and imaginative children. She took great notes and asked terrific questions and we got some solid confirmation on some notions and ideas she had gotten herself.

As the reading came to a close, I checked to see if she had anything more to ask of me. Bethany hesitated a bit and said she did have one more thing. She wanted to know how her mother was. She said her mother's name was Sheila. As I connected to my guides again, I immediately sensed that Sheila wasn't in the earth plane any longer. I asked Bethany if Sheila had crossed.

Bethany told me Sheila had passed just six weeks before. As I began to connect with the energy of Sheila, I got a very surprising burst of angry energy. It was almost like someone popped a balloon of anger in my face. I looked at Bethany and cautiously mentioned that I felt her mother had been an angry woman in life and had been fairly spiteful. I will tell you that it is not in my nature to speak ill of anyone's relatives, and had I not been so taken aback by this burst of negative energy, I probably wouldn't have said anything to Bethany.

Surprisingly, when I looked at Bethany, she was nodding in agreement. I closed my eyes to connect to Sheila again and a vision of Archangel Michael appeared between Shelia and me.

It is common for me to call on Archangel Michael before I do any readings. I ask him for protection and to sever any cords of attachment that I may obtain during a reading. In as many years as I have called on him, he has only appeared a few times, but never in this way nor has he ever spoken to me. This time was different.

Michael stood tall and strong between us, the tip of his mighty sword was pointed to the ground. He said to me, *"Susan, you are not to connect to this energy"*.

As I looked past Michael, I could see Sheila and I could see two angels standing in the background watching her. She was so angry and her energy was swirling like a storm. The surprising thing was that those two angels were completely grey. They weren't vibrating at any color, they were just grey.

Quickly, the image of my guide "Garrod" came through to me and said, *"Susan, you can't connect to her. She hasn't crossed, yet"*.

I was horrified. Shocked and taken aback, I asked Garrod, *"Why hasn't she crossed and what is happening to her?"*

Garrod waved a sense of peace over me and said calmly, *"We have her. We see her. Sheila chooses not to cross. We cannot force her. It is her free will. She has taken her life in anger and in spite. She chooses to stay in that energy. The angels are with her and will take her when she is ready. We will not leave her."*

I was completely confused and said, " *Garrod, the angels are grey."*

"Yes, dear one, she has not accepted or aligned her energy to the angels. She turns from their help. They will not leave her." he responded calmly to my frenetic state.

Confused and a little dazed, I asked Garrod, *"What am I going to tell her daughter? Do I tell her that her mother hasn't crossed? That can't be good, can it? Am I to deliver that message to her?"*

Garrod waved his hand in front of my face (I think he thinks he is a Jedi) and gently said, *"Tell her child that Sheila is with angels."*

As Garrod faded from view, I told Bethany her mother was with angels, and it was too soon for me to connect with her. I suggested she come back in a few months to see if we could talk to her then.

When I looked back at Bethany, she was looking at me with a chill in her eyes which startled me. Bethany told me Sheila was indeed an angry and spiteful woman. She had lied to, and manipulated, Bethany for most of her life, alienating her from the rest of the family. Bethany had tried to rekindle relationships with her family, but Sheila would do everything in her power to sabotage it. When Bethany had finally had enough, and told her mother she needed to take a break to think about her life and her relationships, Sheila took her own life as punishment for Bethany.

Bethany is a lovely soul. She is a healer and a very intuitive woman. As she left my company, I sat down and prayed she would find her Universal purpose in the gifts she has been given. I also pray that Sheila turns to those grey angels and allows them to vibrate the color and frequency she needs to move to a place of love and forgiveness. I hope she lets them take her by her hands and together they walk into that bright light to begin her healing.

In all of the readings I have done for suicide victims, this reading was the closest thing to a "hell" that I have ever seen. I am surprised by it. I understand, free will holds a great deal of importance for a soul. The self-inflicted purgatory this soul had created for herself seemed to be another lesson in self-forgiveness.

Loving everyone, especially you, is the most important thing of all. Forgiveness comes from love. God is Love. Love is our salvation.

Gene

The final piece of the puzzle came unexpectedly and wildly. I will tell you, this reading is right up there among my favorite experiences …ever. It was my rock and roll finale and it couldn't have been any more perfect, really. Sometimes, God or the Universe gives me some awesome presents. I will tell you that this reading is one of those great gifts.

I am keeping this story as true to life as I can without identifying the people involved. I feel like too much manipulation will wreck the message, and we can't miss this message. It rocks…just like the awesome man who delivered it.

The job of being a psychic/medium offers the opportunity to meet some pretty incredible, and sometimes famous people both living and deceased. Unfortunately, many famous people come with confidentiality statements. So, you can't ever say, "Hey! I read for (insert celebrity name) and he/she is awesome!"…or, "(insert celbrity name) is just bat shit crazy!" Whichever the case may be, you signed a paper which clearly stated you wouldn't share any information with anyone other than your cosmic posse.

One of my favorite clients, in particular, is a very famous internationally known and loved person. Every time I see this celebrities products on the store shelves, I feel like I should get a family discount. I can't say it, but you know I am thinking it LOUDLY.

This last reading and last bit of information was for the wife of a well known rock and roll guitar player. She is incredible, in her role as rock wife and super mommy. I completely admire and respect her, and I am envious of the way she balances her coolness with her attention to organizational detail. She totally gets the need for balance, in everything. She is successful because she embraces the good and the bad in herself, and in everyone and everything else. The best part is, she has no idea that she has wrangled what everyone else strives for and she didn't even try. She is the personification of awesomeness.

On the night I had scheduled her reading, I didn't get home until almost eight in the evening. Amy had left me a couple of Facebook messages telling me she had paid and was ready whenever I was. The weather had not been co-operative and I was frazzled from my hour-long drive home from the Phoenix and Dragon Bookstore, during a thunderstorm.

When I finally got home, I grabbed my notebook, a pen, a diet coke and headed for the office. As I dialed the phone, I said a quick prayer that Amy wouldn't be mad at me, or at least not very mad. I was so relieved when Amy answered the phone and was as sweet as she could be. Well, relieved, and surprised, since I was at least half an hour late.

The reading started off as usual with Amy's guides giving me information Amy needed to pay attention to. Most of it was about her child, and how smart and different he was. It was a pleasant reading and about midway through, Amy asked me if I could see if anyone wanted to connect with her from the other side. No one had come through in the beginning, but sometimes concentrating a little extra energy will assist those on the other side to come through more easily.

I went back into connection, took a deep breath and immediately an energy came forward that caused me to giggle out loud during my exhale. The energy of this person was like a great party. Warm and loving, and a whole lot of fun, but no real physical description or vision was happening. However, I could tell it was a male energy. I told Amy I had a younger guy coming through whose energy was making me laugh.

I could hear Amy chuckle on the other end of the phone. As I linked to the energy of her laughter, into my mind's eye came the vision of a large, crazy haired, frenetic rocker dude. He was laughing and his lovely eyes were twinkling with love and admiration for Amy, but mostly for her son. His energy was wonderful. It was like taking a bath in love. I know that sounds crazy, but really, this guy was the epitome of big crazy love. I was digging it, in totality.

As I began describing this large man and his very creative look, Amy knew immediately who I was talking about and remarked how she had been hoping he would come through. I told Amy he gave me a headache and I thought he had died from a head injury. She told me they weren't sure if that was true, no one knew what had actually killed him. She told me he had jumped from his eighth floor hotel room. He had committed suicide.

I was stunned. This man had committed suicide and there were no angels. I asked Amy how long ago was his death. She told me that it was only a couple of years ago.

No angels.

There was only this happy charismatic man with

huge energy, who was loving in great, huge ways. This was hardly what I was used to seeing in a suicide reading. I was confused and bewildered. Everything I had ever been shown was now in question. I didn't get it. So, I did what I normally do. I went on with the reading and decided to ask my guides about it later.

Amy told me this wonderful soul had been named Gene. Gene went on and on about how wonderful Amy's son was. He beamed bright pink love as he expressed his pride of this exceptional little boy. I asked Amy, if her son knew of Gene.

"Gene was my Manny." She explained. He took care of the baby while Amy and her husband worked. I had never heard the term "manny", but I got it. Man+Nanny=Manny

Looking at the man who was standing before me, with his huge rocker persona, he seemed very little like a nanny, but the love he was radiating showed me that he had been incredible at it.

Gene gave me several things to tell Amy and her husband, mostly about forgiveness. Gene had been a care giver and a nurturer. He was sensitive, far too sensitive to live in this harsh world. He had created a solid front of being a big, tough, rocker on the outside, but it wasn't enough to protect his soft inside. Mix that with a little inherited mental illness and you could see why his path had ended the way it did. Although his death was a great shock to everyone who loved him, it wasn't a shock to me. I have seen souls like Gene, many times; special souls who are designed to love and feel in ways which are specifically needed to complete their earthly purpose, yet all too often they are not strong enough for the cruelties of this life.

Gene loves hard and he is loved hard.

It was a great reading and Gene talked a lot about his brother and all of the people he was trying to help from the other side. He explained how he was better able to help from over there, and how he finally felt like he was doing what he was supposed to do. His death brought to him a new life of healing, and loving, and helping people.

He told Amy it was important for her, and for her husband, to learn to love themselves and forgive themselves, completely. He made a point of telling us how imperative it is to get that done while we are here on the earth plane.

We laughed a lot during that reading and talked about a spider tattoo which I thought belonged to Gene.

Amy immediately laughed when I mentioned the spider tattoo. Amy told me how Gene loved spiders. He would never kill one. If one of those scary things were in the house and was freaking out the women folk, Gene would simply, scoop up the offending party and set it free outside. It was such a joke between all of Gene's friends, that Amy had gotten a spider tattoo just to honor Gene's love. Gene totally claimed it. So, I guess it really was Gene's tattoo, but Amy was wearing it!

We went over our allotted reading time that evening, neither of us wanting to disconnect from the fabulous energy of Gene. When I finally closed connection, we thanked Gene for coming through and I said my goodbye's to Amy. When I hung up the phone, I realized I was exhausted. A full day of readings, driving in the storm and then channeling for the last hour, or so, had worn me out.

I sat downstairs, watched some television and had a cup of tea. A few hours later, I went upstairs and took a quick sea salt shower and went to bed. I slept hard, for three hours. I woke up around 3:30 and had to go to the bathroom. As I was going back to sleep, Gene popped into my energy again. Standing there smiling at me, he seemed to want to talk.

"*Gene, I appreciate you, but the reading is over, man.*" I said silently.

Gene wouldn't go away. So, I figured I may as well use this time to ask about the angels. I figured Gene would know about that, as well as anyone. So, I asked Gene if he really had committed suicide. He nodded yes. I told him it didn't make sense to me because he came forward without the now familiar angels.

Was I right about the angels? Gene again, nodded yes.

At this time my main guide Garrod came through to me and said, "*Susan, ask the question for which you seek the answer.*"

So... I asked, "*Gene, if you committed suicide, where are your angels? Why are you alone?*"

Gene wriggled a bit, like a kid who had just been told they could open a present.

Here is what he said:

"*I did have those angels, times two. They carried me to the healing place. When I got there, I took a good look around, at everyone and everything there. There was so much love. It was intense. I figured out pretty quickly that the way for me to heal was by being able to love and forgive myself, and everyone else. So, I got right on that. I worked hard to forgive everyone. I worked hard on forgiving myself. It wasn't easy, but I did it. I did it as fast as I could and it worked. I focused on love. I worked hard on loving me and everyone else. I worked and worked and then, it came naturally, almost like I had never done it any other way. I got through it quickly, compared to other souls. So, now I am here. I am still in the healing place, only now I do my best to show other people how to do it. I am helping them to heal, as I am healing myself. This is my purpose. I feel awesome about it."*

After saying that to me, Gene smiled as big as he could and faded out of my mind. I whispered a thank you to Gene, as I realized I had just been given the final installment for this book and for my own healing. That was intense, as Gene put it. Intense love and intense purpose for one intense rock star of a soul.

I am grateful to Amy, and to Gene, for allowing me to see this and for sharing it with me. I am grateful to be sharing it with you. I hope it helps you understand how your loved ones are okay, and so are you.

You see, it's all about the love and it's all in our own hands. The love from above heals us, as the love from below heals them. We are all connected.

Love is the energy which heals and holds us all. We deserve it. We need it. We provide it. We must learn to accept it from others and most of all, from ourselves. Thank you again, Gene. I will sing your song forever. Keep on rocking, my friend.

Brian

Even though the story of Brian's suicide has been talked about throughout the book, I feel like I should share the whole story of what lead up to his suicide and then the resulting visitation from him. It is hard to talk about, and even though there is really nothing remarkable or earth moving about the visit, it does mark the beginning of a healing process for at least two souls; me, still here on this earth, and him, in the realm we call heaven. It marks the starting place for both of us to heal, move forward, understand, forgive and support one another. It marks the beginning for a new way of thinking, loving and caring about everything. What seemed like a tragic ending was really just the start of our journey to building a new paradigm based on love.

Here is Brian's and my, story:

Once Sondra and I had met in person, we became even closer. Talk of my moving to Atlanta was a daily occurrence. Sondra was offering me an opportunity to leave my high-stress, low-paying job, move to Atlanta and become a full-time psychic. It was truly a dream come true. I didn't want to miss that chance. I felt like I had worked hard toward it.

Megan was soon to be 21. She would be eligible to

go into a group home and find some independence of her own. I had raised Megan for 20 years, and I didn't think it was a bad thing to ask her father to take over for a few months, until we could find a great place for Megan.

I began planning for the move, to Atlanta, in January 2010. The first person I called to plan with was Brian. I figured he would be the one who would be most affected by the move. I wanted to give him the option to vote on the whole thing, before I made any solid decisions.

Brian knew I had been doing psychic readings in the evenings and on weekends, for several years. I explained to him that I had a chance to move to Atlanta, to read full-time and to concentrate on writing. I was shocked at how supportive he was. I asked him to move our daughter in with him for a few months, after I moved, so I could get settled and find the right programs for her. Brian agreed to do it, without a hesitation, without a blink. He said it was fine and he was happy to help me.

I was relieved, and grateful. But, something felt a little shallow about his enthusiasm. Eager to move and begin this new life, I ignored the tiny red flag waving in the back of my head and forged on in happy, ignorant bliss.

Ok…before I go any further, let me rewind the movie a little, just for history's sake.

Brian and I married when I was 22 and he was 33. A year later, he started working for a large software engineering firm. He worked for that firm for 17 years. Three years short of retirement, they fired him.

"Cutbacks", they said.

"Bullshit", I said.

It didn't take a genius to figure out Brian was a high insurance cost to the company. Megan's medical expenses were outrageous, with all of her medications, surgeries, therapies, and specialized doctors. Brian had heart issues and was on daily medication for it.

The straw that broke the camel's back had come in November. I went in for my first mammogram and it had come back abnormal. I had to have additional tests and I would be required to undergo routine mammograms every six months. I am sure the good people, at this large conglomerate, wigged-out at the thought of having to pay even more for Brian and his family. So, like many big corporations, they disconnected from the humanity and went with the numbers.

They fired Brian on December 23rd and cancelled our health insurance the same day, not giving Brian the standard thirty day grace period, leaving us without any kind of health insurance, and no option for Cobra coverage, for several weeks. I honestly can't imagine how anyone could be so heartless, as to leave a handicapped child with a seizure disability and her parents hanging out there with no insurance during the holidays, when stress is high and travel is necessary.

By the grace of God, we didn't have any issues that Christmas. I was grateful for that much. But, I seethed inside and I wanted Brian to sue them. He didn't think it was something he wanted to do.

Brian never got another job. He never recovered from being fired. Eventually, he stopped paying child support. And, four years later, he had completely run out of money. He quit getting his hair cut. He quit eating. He quit taking his heart medications. He quit living in the real world. He quit life, but he didn't quit Megan. He loved his girl and she loved him. He never missed a weekend with her. Megan was always ready to go with him.

I saw Brian deteriorating. I often asked if he needed anything. He always shook his head in response. When I asked Brian to take Megan, for those months, he seemed fine with it. Megan got a small monthly stipend from social security. I hoped with the money coming into the house, combined with the purpose of having to take care of Megan, Brian might perk up again.

I had set the date for the big move on May 21st, 2010. I called Brian on the Wednesday before, to get our schedules synchronized. He answered the phone in a happy enough tone, but when I told him I wanted to leave at 4:30 that Friday, he whimpered a weak "okay". I didn't go any further with the conversation, fearing he was going to back out on me. I had already given my notice at work and was all ready to go. There was no turning back for me at that point.

Friday finally arrived, and the workday was slow. My Honda Civic was packed to the roof with only a small space reserved for me to drive. I was nervous, excited, and ready to begin a new life, in a new city. When I finally finished all that I needed to get completed, it was close to 4:00PM. As I left my office, for the last time, I mentally crossed the last task off of the "pre-move to do list". I took a deep breath and left that old building for the last time.

My original plan was to leave straight from work and head to Atlanta, as Brian was supposed to pick up Megan from the nurse/ sitter at 4:30. Meg and I had already said our good-byes that morning, but something told me to go spend a few more minutes with her and to connect with Brian before I left. I went back to the house to spend my last few minutes in Kentucky with Megan. When I got there, I said my good-byes to our nurse/sitter and she went on her way. I sat with Megan, talked more about what was happening and we loved on one another.

When I looked at the clock it was 4:45 and Brian hadn't arrived. In the twenty years I had known Brian, I could count on one hand the number of times he had been late. Panic began to set in and it started to dawn on me, he wasn't coming. Trying not to give up hope, I imagined he was just confused about the schedule. His normal time to pick up Megan was usually around 6:30. I tried to call him and he didn't answer. I imagined he had already left. He had recently disabled his cell phone to only call out for emergency, so I couldn't contact him on it.

Doing my best to stay positive, I took advantage of this time to pack a few more things and stay a little longer with Megan. Six thirty came and went, and he hadn't arrived nor answered his phone. I left several messages on his answering machine, but in my heart I already knew what he had done.

I tried to call his parents to see if they knew where he had gone, or if they had spoken to him that day. They didn't answer the phone. I left a message, telling them Brian had not picked up Megan and I hadn't been able to reach him. Finally, at 8:00 and in complete desperation, I left Megan with a friend and drove an hour north to Dayton, Ohio, where Brian lived.

I hadn't been to that house in over ten years. The area had changed a great deal since I had been there last and between those changes and my fear, it was a challenge to find my way.

When I pulled up, there were already two police cars with lights flashing, near the driveway. Brian's parents were standing in the yard and his mother was sobbing. My heart slammed into my stomach. He had done it, the ultimate passive-aggressive act.

We stayed in the front yard for several minutes, until a news crew shined lights in our faces and the police escorted us into the house.

When I went into the house, I asked the officers if I could get my daughter's paperwork. They didn't have a problem with it. So, I went back into the bedroom. I noticed my clothes were still in the closet. My pictures still hung on the walls. A small crown, from a musical, I had placed on an ironing board, ten years before, was still right where I left it. Even though there was no clutter to be seen, a thick coat of dust lay on every surface, coating everything like grey flannel.

Brian had always kept his drapes drawn tightly, which was something we argued about during our marriage. After I left, he never opened them at all, it seemed. The mix of dust and moisture made the house smell like it was underground. He had stopped living. This house was like a tomb. The only food in the house was Megan's favorites. Her bedroom was neat and tidy and dust free.

The sight of all if it made my head reel, the reality of what was happening numbed me. His parents had seen these things, every week, for years. Why didn't they do something to help him? Why didn't I ever come back here to check?

I stayed there, at the house, as long as I was needed, but I had to get back to Megan, back to Kentucky.

When I went to bed that night, Brian appeared immediately. He was being held up by two massive blood-red angels. Brian's head was huge and his face seemed to hang down in an odd way. His body was just a small nub wrapped up in a dark red printed fabric. I could feel him being sorry. I could feel him begging me, for my forgiveness.

I was angry. I turned my back to him and said, "There is no forgiveness for you here, you son of a bitch. I tore up my life to make a new one, and you said it was safe to do it. I asked you FIRST. You supported me. You were fine with it. Now, what am I going to do?" He just stood there, held up by those two emotionless angels. His head hung down and the energy of his pain radiating from him, like a blue mist. I could feel his remorse. I could feel his sorrow. My heart wanted desperately to feel sorry for him and forgive him; it wanted to move him into a place of love. However, there was a sharp and pointed part of me that wanted to hate him and punish him even more. The angels moved him out of my energy. I slept, fitfully, for the few hours until morning.

It took months to be able to calmly look at his visitation. His energy was so low he couldn't hold it together to fully manifest. He was so down and depressed that his energy was only at the most basic survival level. He had no foundation. He had lost himself. Brian had to start at the beginning and build it back up. I didn't see him again for a long while. Of course, I blamed myself for every little bit of it, but I have laid that aside. He made that decision. I didn't get to vote. I forgive him today. I do.

He still comes to me on occasion, mostly at night. I know he saw Megan graduate. I know he watches her in her new home and new workshop. I believe he is helping both of us and I am grateful for that.

I know he's getting the love, understanding, and care that he didn't get here on earth. I'm grateful for that too. I'm also grateful he came through on that first night. I know how much energy it must have taken, and how hard he had to try to do it. I am sorry I turned my back to him. I forgive us both. I love us both and even through all of this, I am grateful for my time with him.

Be at peace Brian and thank you for all you have given to Megan and me. Thank you for looking out for us and making sure we landed in safe places. Megan and I both love you and miss you, even if we still get a little mad at you.

Susan Rushing

CHAKRA KHAN, LET ME LOVE YOU

I have a wonderful "root friend" named Cynthia. She is a very gifted energy worker and a darned fine massage therapist. I like to call her Chakra Kahn, because she is all about the chakra system and keeping it well cared for. Calling her Chakra Kahn makes her smile too, and that is one of my favorite things to do. If you are reading this and saying to yourself, "What the "h" is a chakra?" Just hang on; I am going to explain it, in just a minute. It's not complicated, but it is something you should know about healing on an energetic level. Healing on the energetic level will help you heal on the emotional and physical level too ... mind, body, spirit, the balance of the big three.

If you already know all about chakras and you are a veritable Chakra Khan yourself, then feel free to move on to the next section of this book. I am probably not going to tell you anything you don't already know. If you are not interested in energy healing or do not believe in energy healing, I will tell you to feel free to move on to the next section, as well. If your religious views are standing in the way of you learning about energy medicine, it's okay. Let me remind you that there are many instances of hands-on healing in the bible. "Laying on of hands" has been a religious practice for thousands of years; same thing, different words. Jesus did it. His mother, Mary, did it. Mary Magdalene did it, then took to it France and taught it. Energy healing is the way to heal a soul. I am going to relay this information to you, as I know it. As I learned it, from my Appalachian Grandfather, who showed me how to feel energy, from my work, as an energy worker and a psychic, and also from all of the research I have done.

When I talk to my clients about their chakras and they want to learn more, I always point them to the internet for some basic advice. After all, there is no need to reinvent the wheel, and if you can learn all about the wheel for free, that's even better. If a client is determined to buy a book, I just point them to the chakra center of the bookstore and let them peruse the shelves, for a book which resonates with them.

As for my book, just a basic understanding is all that's needed. If it becomes like a seed planted in your brain, prompting you to do your own research, it will only help you along in your healing. Gathering information in that way is so much better than having one person tell you how it is and how it's going to be. Develop your own system according to your own research. Build your own paradigm here, too.

I feel for you. I think I love you.

Chakras are all about energy. Our souls are comprised of energy. The flow of positive energy or "chi" is vital to our health and well being. So, basically, the chakra system is comprised of seven energy centers that run through the center of your body. Many people tell you to imagine them as lotus flowers blooming and spinning. Spinning flowers are fabulous, I dig that image. However, when I think of these energy centers and controlling the spin, it helps me if I think of box fans. You know the ones. Your mom might have had them in a window or sitting in the living room floor every summer. You probably got warned not to stick your fingers in there, and got chastised for making your voice all choppy by talking, yelling or singing into them. But for me, fans have knobs…and knobs mean control. Way more helpful for me than spinning flowers.

You have control over your chakras and what they are doing. It takes a little practice and guidance at first, but before too long you will be able to check on your chakra alignment and notice any sluggishness or blockages of energy, on your own.

A quick chakra check and alignment done every day will help you stay in tune with yourself. I know, you just said "Every day?" Yeah, this is one of those psychic protection things you should take care of daily. Think of it like brushing your teeth, except you are brushing your energy. It's just good psychic hygiene.

You may also want to seek out an energy worker (like a Reiki practitioner), for a good tune up two or three times a year, more if you feel you need it. I always figure it is good to have another set of eyes, or one really good third eye, to look you over. An energy worker can identify disturbances or blockages in the flow of your energy, and what has contributed to those blockages. If you are recovering from being affected by suicide, just remember that big emotional and traumatic events can cause energy blockages and deficiencies. Identifying the location of the blockage or deficiency is like a little inside information about what is really going on with you. It gets past your analytical mind and straight into the source and cause of what is bothering you, and it will give you something to focus your energy on while you are healing. An energy worker can channel energy into the places of need and help you focus your energy on releasing the emotion which holds the blocks in place; he or she will also be able to help you remove those blockages.

Where do these people get this miraculous energy? They get it from the same source as the people healing on the other side. Whatever your belief system, whether it be God, Spirit or Universal Energy, it is the same big love. Love is real. Love heals.

The Seven Main Chakra Centers

As I said, there are seven major chakras which run vertically along the center of your body, starting at the base of your trunk and ending at the crown of your head. By working with these energu centers and keeping them aligned, you can heal faster and understand yourself better than ever. Being in tune and knowing your energy systems is really about getting in touch with your higher self. Your higher self is in direct contact with your guides and angels.

It's important to note, we are dealing with vibrations when it comes to healing energy. Without getting into a whole quantum physics discussion, let me say simply: everything has a vibration. If we can find the vibration needed to heal a block or deficiency in our energy, we can provide a supplement to the area by using sound and colors which vibrate to that frequency. The angels who came through during the suicide readings helped me recognize this. They vibrated at the frequency needed by the soul to complete the task. For instance, Brian's angels were red, the color of the root chakra. The root chakra is about basic survival and being grounded to the earth. He needed that particular frequency. Brian was at the lowest, basic level of soul survival. Those angels were vibrating at the frequency required to support him.

We can support ourselves in the same way, with those colors and with sounds. Sound is a vibration. I am going to give you the colors, notes, and some affirmations to use in healing, as it relates to each chakra. As I tell everyone, use what feels right to you and throw out the rest. It's your belief system. I will tell you, staying in touch with my higher self and understanding my energetic health have been the keys to keeping my dragon on a short leash.

So, let's start at the beginning and work our way up:

The Root Chakra

The first of the seven major chakras is the Root Chakra, also known as Muladhara. Muladhara grounds us to the Earth; it is positioned at the perineum and faces downwards towards the Earth. This chakra is involved with the realm of physical and material; and when this chakra is opened, it brings a feeling of wholeness and contentment. When it is balanced it you feel strong and vital. This chakra's basic function is to ground you. It gives you the feeling that you have a right to be here … a right to exist. If the root chakra becomes unbalanced, blocked or compromised then physical symptoms can occur, like obesity, sciatica, and more. Blockages can come about by unwillingness to move on, change direction, or by being resistant to needed changes.

The root chakra vibrates to the color red, which stimulates and energizes. Visualizing the color red during meditation can be used as a method to heal or revitalize this chakra. If you don't meditate, that is okay. Look at red things. Wear red clothes. Eat red foods. Basic issues of childhood, security, poverty, emotional abandonment, father issues can all be held in this chakra.

This chakra vibrates to the musical note "C".

Root Chakra Affirmations:

I am here.

I am strong.

I am vital.

I belong.

I am abundant.

I am grounded in the love for life on earth.

Note: Okay, these little affirmations will be helpful whether you believe in chakra energy or not. If you find you have one or more of the listed issues or ailments, or if you realize you hold discontent in one of the listed areas: Stand in front of a mirror once a day and look yourself straight in the eye and repeat the affirmation. Say it like you mean it. Do it a couple of times, if you feel that you need to. You will notice a change.

The Sacral Chakra

The second chakra is the Sacral Chakra or Svadisthana.

Svadisthana vibrates to the color orange.

The Sacral Chakra is located halfway between the pubic area and the navel, and pretty much stays dormant until puberty. It's considered to be the storage center for energy coming and going throughout the body. It concentrates on the energy from the external world like wealth, sexual power, self-gratification and creativity. This chakra is nourished by developing support systems, setting parameters and boundaries. Its purpose is reproduction and creation. The basis of the Sacral Chakra is the right to feel; the ability to communicate and comprehend basic emotions. If this basic right is desecrated; impotence, frigidity, uterine, bladder, or kidney issues can and will occur. Issues which can be housed in this chakra are: mother issues, child issues, sexual issues, lover/spouse issues and creativity blockages. The imbalance of giving and taking in relationships is also housed in this chakra and can cause major blockages.

This chakra vibrates to the musical note "D".

Sacral Chakra affirmations:

I unconditionally love and approve of myself, at all times.

I am good enough to have what I want.

I release my negative attitudes which block my experience of pleasure.

I allow abundance and prosperity into my life.

I am in control of my own sexuality.

I give myself permission to enjoy my sexuality fully.

I love myself unconditionally and without question, just the way I am, right now.

Note: It might be hard to look at yourself, in the mirror, and say these things. I was surprised at how difficult it was to look into my own eyes and express loving thoughts to myself. Sad, but true. If you find the same truth for yourself, you can start in a small way. When you go to the bathroom, or when you look in your rear-view mirror, look in your eyes for a couple of seconds and say your name followed by "I love you". Then move on, you don't need to linger if it is uncomfortable. If you keep it up it will soon be fine. We have been taught that it is selfish to love ourselves. It isn't selfish. It's vital.

The Solar Plexus Chakra

The third chakra is in the Solar Plexus and is also called Manipura. This is your power center.

It is located in the abdomen, about 4 inches above your belly button.

The solar plexus chakra vibrates to the color yellow.

This chakra gathers and holds life-force energy or chi.

Manipura's basic function deals with willpower and personal power, as well as self-determination. The Solar Plexus gives us the right to act, to be innovative and free. If it becomes blocked or compromised it can bring about ulcers, diabetes, eating disorders, and blood sugar issues.

Issues which can be housed in this chakra will have to do with personal power. High accountability in childhood, abuse issues, violence, and control issues can all bring about poor flow in this area.

This chakra vibrates to the musical note "E".

Solar Plexus Chakra affirmations:

I love and respect myself at all times.

I trust my worthiness.

There are no failures.

I learn from everything I do.

I listen to and trust my deepest insights.

I am worthy of the very best in life.

I release judgment and know everything is perfect, as it is.

I am powerful in being me.

No one takes my power; I am the keeper of me.

And, my personal favorite ... I am freaking FIERCE, in the most loving and respectful way.

The Heart Chakra

The fourth chakra is the Heart Chakra, also known as Anahata. It is the center of the heart. Not too hard to figure that one out, huh?

Anahata vibrates to the color green. I sometimes see this energy as pink, when someone is radiating unconditional love.

This chakra is located in the center of the chest and its function is all about love, devotion, compassion, joy and healing. It helps us manifest love and forgiveness, and is nourished by finding passion in life. Its focus is our basic right to love and be loved. If wounded or blocked, it can cause asthma, blood pressure issues, heart disease, and lung disease, due to a lack of confidence in self, closing down, or feelings of being taken for advantage.

Issues which can be housed in the heart chakra can be: Well, basically anything that breaks your heart or takes your joy.

The heart chakra vibrates to the musical note "F".

Heart Chakra affirmations:

I am adequate at all times to do everything required of me.

I love who I am.

I am willing to love everything about myself.

I trust in love.

I open my heart to love.

I forgive myself

I forgive those who need forgiving, for not being what I wanted them to be.

Love is the purpose of my life.

Love is everywhere.

I open myself to the healing powers of love.

I am confident the healing power of Universal love will heal my mind, heart, and body.

Note: Love, love, love, love, love…it is the only real thing. Take it. Give it. Make it and Live it. It's like the best organic produce for the soul.

The Throat Chakra

The fifth chakra is the Throat Chakra. It is also called Vishuddha.

The throat chakra vibrates to the color of a clear blue sky.

This chakra represents verbal communication and speech development. It deals with issues of personal expression and how others see us.

We nourish this chakra through creativity and expression. Its basic right is to speak and hear the truth, including all transgressions. If this is violated and we are not allowed to communicate or have issues in communication, disease and blockages like sore throats, swollen glands, colds, and thyroid problems may occur. Please remember that communication is not just about talking. It is about expressing. If you are a singer, you must sing. If you are a painter, you must paint. How you express yourself is as individual as a fingerprint.

Issues which can be housed in the Throat Chakra can be; denying personal truths, not speaking your truth, allowing others to speak for us, stifling creativity, and verbal abuse.

This chakra vibrates to the musical note "G".

Throat Chakra affirmations:

I substitute love, joy, and creative expression for old patterns of addiction and abuse.

I willingly give up (smoking, alcohol abuse, drug abuse, overeating and unhealthy dieting) to enhance my own creative gifts.

It is now safe for me to express my feelings.

I love and trust my creative gifts.

It is right for me to express the best of who I am now.

I release all fear and doubts which block the way to my creative expression.

Note: Singing in the car may make you look crazy, to other drivers, but will keep you from going there for real. It works for me, baby. Sing the body electric; celebrate the you yet to come. (that's from Fame, just in case you wondered.)

The Third Eye Chakra

The sixth chakra is the Third Eye/ Brow Chakra, also known as Ajna.

It vibrates to the color Indigo.

I have been told, if the color indigo is worn, it will balance this chakra. That sounds really handy. I just have one little problem. I always have an issue with knowing what color Indigo actually is. I went to the internet for clarification. I found way too many choices. So, I settled for an old and reliable friend; my crayon box. I looked through the blues until I found the indigo crayon.

Indigo in my best description is a deep blue with a touch of violet. You may have chosen that color as a youngster, to draw a night sky, or to color someone's blue jeans.

The third eye chakra directly relates to issues of discipline, emotional maturity, wisdom and discernment. You may have heard people talking about their third eye in psychic circles. It's true that it is recognized as your psychic center and is thought to be the hub for intuition and insight.

Situated in the middle of the forehead, just above the brow line, it functions as the entrance to spiritual ways of thinking, psychic awareness, and extrasensory perception. It gives you the basic right to see. If this chakra is blocked or compromised; poor memory, inadequate vision, weak mental clarity, failure to differentiate patterns, denial, nightmares, hallucinations, and headaches can manifest. Issues of trust, crisis, violence, developing a fear of the unknown, and denial of psychic ability can all be housed in the third eye chakra.

This chakra vibrates to the musical note "A".

Third Eye Chakra affirmations:

I open myself to my intuition and deepest knowing.

I accept and acknowledge my gut feelings and pay heed to them.

I acknowledge I am the source for creating my life the way I would like it to be.

I release all obstacles to my growth and development.

I am open to new ideas, people, and situations which will enhance my joy and happiness.

I re-think all negative thoughts about myself, and others, and choose to see the good and love in everyone.

I create clarity and unlimited vision for myself, and my life.

I trust whatever comes to me is for my greatest joy and highest good.

Note: I have come to understand that sometimes focusing on your third chakra and trusting your power from that perspective can be linked to the third eye chakra. The phrase "trusting your gut" is all about trusting your intuition. Focusing on your gut for answers allows you to empower yourself and claim your intuition in a powerful way.

The Crown Chakra

The seventh and last major chakra is the Crown Chakra, also called Sahasrara.

It is thought to be the focal point of consciousness and is the Master chakra for all of the others. It is the sacred center for human life force energy. I believe this chakra to be the connection to the Divine. This chakra vibrates to a fabulous mixture, the colors of gold, silver, white and violet.

It works with the realm of the spirit and is fed by unconditional love, compassion, and peace.

The crown chakra is positioned at the top of the head and functions as the union to the divine, inspiration, insight, and the collective consciousness and oneness with all. This chakra is our connection to God, Spirit, whatever your belief. It is also our connection with one another.

It gives us the ability to know spiritual truth and to be in line with our higher self. It is said that your spirit self, which is not in this earth plane consciousness is called the higher self. Your higher self knows and wants the very best for you.

By keeping the crown chakra balanced and unblocked you have direct communication with your higher self. Your higher self sits with your guides and angels, so really it's a good thing to keep that line open. If this chakra becomes blocked, confusion, loneliness and isolation can become prevalent.

Life issues which can be housed in this chakra may be: spiritual trust issues, religious guilt, abandonment, disconnection with source, suffering alone.

This chakra vibrates to the musical note "B".

Crown Chakra affirmations:

I love, and I am loved.

Love is the only real thing.

Love makes me free.

I am always willing to take the next step in my life.

I am divinely protected and guided.

I am safe and all life loves and supports me now.

Love surrounds me, protects and nourishes me.

I acknowledge the source of love is within me.

The more love I give the more there is to receive.

I am open to the goodness and abundance of the Universe.

I am love.

So, now you know a little more about the chakra system and you can see how it relates to souls, and the angels who have come through to teach us.

After being shown all of this incredible information and studying the chakra system a little more closely, I realized that healing is all about energy, on the other side. So, it stands to reason, healing the energy of the soul is the best way to heal the energy of the body, the mind and the world.

Ok, we don't have to concentrate on the world right now. Let's just start with you and me.

Susan Rushing

13

WHAT IS GOOD ABOVE IS GOOD BELOW
BUILDING YOUR OWN PARADIGM

I have talked a great deal about a great many things in this book. I did it on purpose. It was my desire to have you look at all the opportunities to rebuild your way of thinking about suicide. I wanted to make it clear, you have the right to believe in a way which feels best to you. You have the right to heal and be loved by yourself and by everyone else. I want you to understand you are a precious commodity to this world. You are loved from above and loved here on earth.

As I began to rebuild my paradigm for healing from Brian's suicide, I realized the healing techniques I had been shown, from the other side, were completely applicable to me here on the Earth plane. That made perfect sense to me. The spirit of Ginny had shown me how we were all made up of energy. Healing my energy was the same as healing my soul.

I had been doing energy work for other people for years, but I had never gone to anyone on a regular basis to have any work done on my energy. Once I began to get regular Reiki sessions, it didn't take long to notice my mood and attitude beginning to change.

My Reiki practitioner helped me clear out the energy of fear, which had been planted in my soul. That work enabled me to begin losing the weight I was using as protection. I was free of the oppressing idea that I was not safe. I *am* safe. I am loved. I am love.

I learned how I was taking on too much of the energy of my clients. My empathy, for the people I read for, was causing me to take on their pain and suffering. Reiki helped me release that energy too. I always feel like a new person after an energy session.

There are a good many energy healing modalities out there. Just like everything else, if you should decide to try it, choose the one which feels best to you. Also, when choosing a practitioner, please follow the guidelines for choosing a psychic or medium. You will find that in the "Social They" chapter.

Having energy work done was just the beginning. The colors of the angels and the realization that those colors corresponded to the energy vibration of the colors of the chakra system was like discovering a great secret which I could use to my benefit.

Those giant angels showed me the importance and the relevance of sound and color as a tool for healing my soul. I began to get creative, using color and shapes, to help communicate and support myself in the areas that felt weakest to me. For instance, when I was feeling less than powerful, I surrounded myself with yellow. The third chakra is our power center and it vibrates to the color yellow. I wore yellow, I ate yellow food. The power of my thoughts, combined with the energy of yellow, was a powerful cocktail to heal my power center.

I also made note of colors I was drawn to. If I was being drawn to shades of pale blue, I sat with myself to see what I needed to talk about. If I seemed to be focusing on pink or green, I knew my heart energy needed some attention. I made sure, I stood in front of the mirror and told myself that I loved me every day.

As crazy as it all seemed, people began to notice a change in the way I acted. My shine was returning. These things may seem crazy, but let me tell you this: just because it's crazy doesn't mean it isn't real. I incorporated this kind of healing into my daily routine. I began to feel like I had control again. Soon, I felt like I *could* get through it all.

One day it dawned on me, I was the light at the end of my own tunnel. I figured, I was just going to have to keep walking through the tunnel until I came to my light. So I did, I kept on walking.

As I began to see the benefit of energy work and self-love in healing from my grief, a surprising thing happened. I began to see other parts of my life fall into place. As I loved and healed myself, I was better able to love and care for the people around me. I was also in a healthier place to begin to heal the relationships that had challenged me in the past. It wasn't all magic, believe me.

There were relationships which could not be healed. I tried, but some loose ends are not meant to be re-tied. It isn't anyone's fault. It is just the way it is. It was a complete surprise when I realized the inability to heal those relationships didn't really matter. Being at a distance from those situations helped me gain a healthier viewpoint.

Some of those old relationships had been toxic, and I was much better off without them. It was a little sad, I admit that. I grieved the loss of those people. However, I sent them on their way surrounded by love. I prayed for them to find happiness and success. I just needed them to do that, far away from me. As I began taking better care of myself, it became clear how sometimes there are people in my life who were either draining or damaging, and it was more than okay for me to love them from a distance. I had a choice of whom and what was going to come into my life.

Miraculously, good things began coming to me. It seems, the happier and more positive I become the happier and more positive my life becomes. When difficult times appear, I am more able to deal with them, in healthy ways. I know I will be okay, because I am the one in charge of making things happen.

All of this self love was doing wonders for me and for my household. I still had a couple of big hurdles to go.

The number one challenge I faced, and really what put the rhinestone collar around my dragon's neck, was gaining the ability to forgive. I know it is hard to forgive someone for kicking your legs out from under you. It is hard to forgive someone who has kicked at you when you were down. It is much easier to stay in a victim mode and blame people for your sadness and tell the world what monsters they are and how they have done you wrong. You can't stay there.

Staying in the victim mode means you will always be a victim. Re-hashing and re-telling makes you live in that energy and you continue to be victimized by them. If you are that mad or sad about what someone has done to you, talk it out one last time. Get a piece of paper and write it down, all of the mean and horrible things you can think of that the person did to you. Make sure you put in all the gasps and heartbreaks and passive aggressive moments of that relationship. Write it all out. Pour out your heart. It's the last time, so do it up good.

When you are done with all of your writing, go outside with the paper and a lighter or a match. In your mind, go back to a good time in the relationship and remember being in that energy. Put yourself in the picture of the memory of your happiest time in that relationship.

When you are feeling good about it, light the paper. Tell the person you forgive them, and ask your angels to come and take the energy on that paper away from you. Release it, so the Universe can heal all of you. Release it. Release your anger and hurt. Release it, to regain your power. Remember, *you* are the powerful one in this.

If the anger comes up again, it's okay. Just do the ritual again. Sometimes it takes a few times to get something like that out of your system. It works for me, baby.

Forgiving other people is the very best way to start forgiving you. Self-forgiveness was a difficult thing for me. As a confirmed and self-acknowledged control freak, I felt it was important to claim every ounce of responsibility for Brian's death. I beat myself up about it, every minute of every day, for a couple of years. Forgiving Brian came with some difficulty. I really had to set my mind to it.

Forgiving others who were rude or hateful wasn't all that hard. In fact, it wasn't hard for me to come from a place of love towards other people at all. But, when it came down to coming from love, towards me, I had a very difficult time. I struggled and struggled with guilt. I just knew the whole thing was on me. If only I had said something. If only I had seen something. If only I had done something.

Then, from out of the blue, came that rock and roll angel named Gene. He was so happy to tell me the secret of how to heal from suicide. He understood it so quickly. Forgiving and loving every one and myself, was the key to freedom. It was the key to being free of the emotional, mental and spiritual baggage which threatened to drag me down into a sea of despair. I am thankful to Gene, for bringing the message in a way that was easy for me to hear and take to heart. I understand the energy it takes for a spirit to manifest with such clarity. I am thankful we were on the same frequency that night, and that his message was good, and crisp, and clear.

Forgiving myself was still hard to do. It *is* still hard to do. I work on it every day. But, by focusing on coming from a place of love and acceptance, and with the belief that we are all connected, it gives me strength. I hope I am becoming a better person with every day that passes.

Living through a loved one's suicide is a difficult and heart-wrenching challenge. But, you can love yourself through it. I'm going to love you through it. That is for sure.

I hope this book has given you enough information and opportunity for you to be able to begin healing and working toward the love and forgiveness which will set you free, as well. It is all about the love.

Use that love to free yourself completely and to whip that dragon's behind…in the most forgiving and loving way possible.

Susan Rushing

ABOUT THE AUTHOR

Susan Rushing is a generational psychic, medium, energy worker and intuitive graphologist, living and working in Atlanta, Georgia. For more information regarding Susan's work please visit the following web sites.

susanrushing.com

phoenixanddragon.com

Susan Rushing

Suicide from the Other Side

Susan Rushing

Made in the USA
Charleston, SC
18 September 2013